DSW 8002

Advanced Knowledge of Social Work

CAPELLA UNIVERSITY

To order books or for customer service, please call 1(800)-CALL-WILEY (225-5945).

Printed in the United States of America.

ISBN 978-0-470-76770-2

Printed and Bound by EPAC Technologies, Inc.

10 9 8 7 6 5 4

Contents

THE BLACKWELL COMPANION TO SOCIAL WORK

Third Edition

Edited by Martin Davies

BLACKWELL PUBLISHING
350 Main Street, Malden, MA 02148-5020, USA
9600 Garsington Road, Oxford OX4 2DQ, UK
550 Swanston Street, Carlton, Victoria 3053, Australia

First edition published 1997
Second edition 2002
Third edition published 2008 by Blackwell Publishing Ltd

1   2008

Library of Congress Cataloging-in-Publication Data

The Blackwell companion to social work/edited by Martin Davies. – 3rd ed.
    p. cm.
    Includes bibliographical references and indexes.
    ISBN 978-14051-7004-8 (pbk. : alk. paper)   1. Social service–Great Britain.
I. Davies, Martin, 1936–

    HV245.B53 2008
    362.3'20941–dc22

                        2007025832

A catalogue record for this title is available from the British Library.

Set in 10 on 12 pt Sabon
by SNP Best-set Typesetter Ltd., Hong Kong
Printed and bound in Singapore
by Markono Print Media Pte Ltd

The publisher's policy is to use permanent paper from mills that operate a sustainable forestry
policy, and which has been manufactured from pulp processed using acid-free and elementary
chlorine-free practices. Furthermore, the publisher ensures that the text paper and cover board
used have met acceptable environmental accreditation standards.

For further information on
Blackwell Publishing, visit our website:
www.blackwellpublishing.com

CHAPTER 1.3

Domestic Violence

Cathy Humphreys

Many social workers work with people affected by domestic violence, but only community sector women's organizations such as Women's Aid respond to women and children survivors as their core business. Intervention to support domestic violence survivors or to challenge domestic violence offenders may only be picked up when they fit into an agency's priorities under a different heading: mental health, substance abuse, child protection, criminal justice.

The 1990s saw renewed attention to domestic violence with an added focus on its impact on children. This move challenged the barrier between the practice focus on child abuse and services perceived to be for women – though Women's Aid refuges have always housed more children than women and employed children's workers from their inception. However, the process of gaining awareness of the needs of children affected by domestic violence has tended to marginalize recognition that domestic violence is a legitimate concern for social workers in adult services as well.

The Extent of the Problem

Problems arise in estimating the scale of domestic violence as it usually happens behind closed doors. Definitions and terminology are always contested, and the term 'domestic violence' has both strengths and limitations:

> *Domestic violence* typically involves a pattern of physical, sexual and emotional abuse and intimidation. . . . It can be understood as the misuse of power and exercise of control by one partner over the other in an intimate relationship, usually by a man over a woman, occasionally by a woman over a man (though without the same pattern of societal collusion) and also occurring amongst same sex couples. It has profound consequences in the lives of individuals, families and communities. (Mullender and Humphreys, 1998, p. 6)

Surveys show large numbers of women affected by domestic violence, usually citing one in four women affected over a lifetime. The British Crime Survey is the most comprehensive UK survey and showed that while many men report some form of abuse, women were overwhelmingly the most chronically abused and the most seriously injured. There were an estimated 635,000 incidents in 2001/2 in England and Wales, of which 81 per cent were attacks on women (Walby and Allen, 2004).

At its most serious, women die: almost two women a week in England and Wales die at the hands of a man with whom they are in or have been in an intimate relationship – accounting for almost half the women who are killed in the country. One-third have separated. It is far rarer for women to kill their male partners or ex-partners and accounts for only 9 per cent of male homicides.

The Effects on Children

The link between child abuse and domestic violence is now well established (Edleson, 2001). Research shows that children living in households where there is domestic violence are more likely to be abused themselves. This suggests that where domestic violence is occurring, questions need to be asked about whether children are also the subject of physical or sexual abuse, and conversely, where there is child abuse, the issue of violence particularly towards the child's mother needs to be explored.

However, the prevalence of direct abuse is difficult to establish. Studies vary widely from 30–66 per cent of child abuse cases (Edleson, 2001). Much depends on whether sensitive questions are asked about domestic violence. For instance, an early study by Gibbons et al. (1995) in an overview of 1,888 child protection referrals across several local authorities, found that in 27 per cent of cases, domestic violence was an issue in the family. However, later studies where staff had been trained to routinely ask questions about domestic violence indicate at least double this figure (Hester, 2006), with two-thirds of children who are the subject of case conferences affected by living with domestic violence (Sloan, 2003).

Similar issues arise in the exploration of child sexual abuse. Farmer and Pollock (1998), in an analysis of 250 children in substitute care who had been sexually abused or sexually abusing, found that 39 per cent came from families where there was domestic violence – primarily violence towards the child's mother. This rate rose to 55 per cent in a more detailed follow-up of 40 children.

Within the framework of domestic violence and post-separation violence, at its most serious, children also die. Child death enquiries, including those associated with deaths during child contact frequently show men who were violent to both the child and the child's mother. Recognition is growing that many children are seriously emotionally affected by living with violence and often witnessing the abuse of one of their parents, usually the mother. The tactics of abuse often represent an attack on the mother–child relationship by the perpetrator, undermining not only his fathering role, but also the mother's parenting abilities. Studies consistently show that children living with chronic domestic violence have two to three times the rates of cognitive and behavioural problems as comparison groups of children from non-violent families. Children who have themselves been physically abused while witnessing acts of violence consistently show the highest levels of behavioural and emotional disturbance. Problems for children can compound over time as developmental stages are disrupted (Rossman, 2001).

Some children, though, show high levels of resilience in the face of their difficult circumstances, and research points to the fact that children have the ability to recover from the effects of violence once they are in a safer, more stable environment. Children who have been most recently exposed to violence tend to show the most marked problems, while those who have moved on and are no longer living with violence may be much less disturbed, both emotionally and behaviourally. These findings have implications for child contact arrangements if violence and abuse towards the child's mother is ongoing.

In summary, then, children's responses to living with domestic violence cannot be predicted. Individualized risk and safety assessments of children and their circumstances need to be undertaken to ascertain the needs and the services which are required.

The Impact on Women

Social workers in mental health teams, disability teams, teams for older people and social workers in the substance use and health sector will all be in touch with women who are affected by domestic violence.

Studies of women and mental health illustrate the seriousness of the impact. Amongst abused women, depression, post-traumatic stress, suicide and self-harm are so prevalent that they can be referred to as 'symptoms of abuse' (Humphreys and Thiara, 2003). Stark and Flitcraft (1996) found that 65 per cent of women had been assaulted within six months of their first suicide attempt. Suicide rates amongst black and minority ethnic women in both the UK and the US are disproportionately high.

The level of problematic substance use (while not a cause of violence) is an issue for a significant number of perpetrators of violence, as it is for some of their victims, though the patterns of use are different. Men are more likely to drink prior to and during an incident and women following an incident often as a means of coping with the emotional and physical pain of abuse (Galvani, 2001).

Other work has highlighted the issues faced by disabled women. A Home Office survey (Mirrlees-Black, 1999) showed 12 per cent of disabled women aged 16–29 had experienced domestic violence in 1995 compared with 8.2 per cent of non-disabled women of the same age. The woman's difficulties in accessing appropriate help, combined with the losses she would incur if she were to separate and the ease with which she could be isolated, increase the power and control of the abuser and compound the impact of abuse.

Women with learning difficulties have been found to be highly vulnerable to domestic violence, and research on the abuse of older people suggests that a proportion of this abuse is the continuation of domestic violence into old age.

Social Work Responses to Domestic Violence

Social workers, particularly those employed in statutory child care, have often been taken to task for:

- ignoring violence towards the child's mother unless the child was directly harmed;
- minimizing the effects on children of witnessing domestic violence;
- focusing on the mother's 'failure to protect' or other problems rather than on the man's violence;
- being slow to recognize the link between domestic violence and child abuse; and
- paying little attention to the specific issues which black women may have in accessing help.

It is easy to blame front-line social work staff for insensitive responses, but accountability for these failings lies with organizations that fail to provide supervision, training and resources for this difficult area of work.

Social workers, like other professionals, have a strong tendency to minimize and avoid violence, and a number of practices have developed amongst social workers which consistently hide domestic violence: see the box below.

Hiding the reality of domestic violence

A study of case files in one local authority's children and families' teams (Humphreys, 2000) showed the ways that domestic violence is concealed:

- Professionals fail to report to child protection conferences known incidents of domestic violence.
- They inappropriately name violence, usually by the man towards the woman, as *marital conflict* or *arguments* so that the source of the danger is not identified and its impact obscured.
- They shift the focus of assessment to other issues such as mental health or alcohol abuse which, while also present, are not the cause of the danger and sometimes result from it.
- They name the mother's behaviour as a problem either equally or more serious than the man's violence, even when there is significant evidence in the file to the contrary.
- They identify the man as the 'cornerstone of the family' rather than challenging his violence towards his partner.
- They only name the most extreme forms of physical violence (the 'atrocity story') while ignoring other aspects of a pattern of emotional, physical and sexual abuse.

Significant organizational problems need to be overcome to develop more effective and safer intervention from social workers where domestic violence is present. Given that there are often both child and adult victim/survivors, policies involving adult and children's services should ensure that there is not an inappropriate focus on one at the expense of the other.

The impediments to women's help-seeking need to be recognized, particularly in relation to social work agencies. Women are often threatened by abusers with the loss of their children or construed as 'mad', bad or unbelievable. Proactive work needs to be undertaken by social workers to overcome discriminatory practices and to be alert to the danger of colluding with the abuser's definition of family problems which invariably invite minimization of the contribution of his violence and maximize the focus on the woman and her shortcomings.

As in many other areas of social work, interagency collaboration is essential. *Working Together* (Department for Education and Skills, 2006c) provides detailed guidance for multi-agency working in the area of domestic violence, while the Children Act 2004 provides the overarching legislative framework through which services to children and families are organized and delivered. A range of multi-agency plans exists in which domestic violence intervention should be featured, and these multi-agency collaborations can provide opportunities for social workers to provide a more responsive and safer service for women and children affected by violence. Attention to confidentiality and safety issues are crucial for good practice: inadvertent leaking of addresses and contact numbers to the abuser may be life-threatening, and concern about it could constrain women from trusting extensive inter-agency referral. Social work training that emphasizes working in partnership with parents may need to be re-thought in circumstances of domestic violence so that the safety of the victim (usually women) and children is not compromised.

It is not only the safety of women and children that needs to be considered. Workers are also at risk, particularly if they shift to a more challenging practice which does not collude with or ignore the perpetrator's violence. Organizations will need both policies and training to implement safety planning into practices of social workers in more self-conscious ways if work in this area is to be progressed.

Future Directions

While there are significant barriers that constrain effective intervention, the increased awareness of domestic violence has led to greater attention to the development of legislation, policy and practice.

A more effective legislative framework is in place with the passing of the Domestic Violence, Crime and Victims Act 2004 and the Protection from Harassment Act 1997. A further development in the UK has been the amendment to the definition of harm in the Adoption and Children Act 2002, which now includes 'impairment suffered from seeing or hearing the ill treatment of another'.

Police have been issued with a clearer mandate for action, including closer supervision of their decisions when called out to incidents of domestic violence. The area of child contact where there has been domestic violence remains problematic. Contradictions can develop between social workers on the one hand urging women to leave to protect their children, and family courts on the other ordering contact which is often unsupervised. Statutory social workers need to develop their practice to ensure that assessments and child protection conference recommendations relevant to private law contact proceedings are communicated clearly to family court practitioners and that women have copies of any relevant assessments, child protection conference minutes and reports.

The re-focusing of children and family services to strengthen family support should allow children and their families affected by domestic violence to have a claim on services (section 17, Children Act 1989). Unfortunately, this right is often tempered by limited resources. Nevertheless, many local authorities now provide funds for children's groups, women's groups, and occasionally for children's workers in refuges, children without recourse to public funds, and short-term payments such as taxi fares to schools and refuges.

Good practice will ensure that social workers are conscious of careful recording and enhanced evidence-gathering in cases of domestic violence. This will mean:

- screening for domestic violence at all stages of referral, investigation and assessment;
- recording in detail any information on domestic violence; and
- case advocacy to ensure that other agencies also document evidence.

A framework of good practice indicators for working with families affected by domestic violence has been developed through work with Women's Aid, social services and four children's charities (Humphreys et al., 2000).

While domestic violence features in the lives of a great many service users seen by social workers, policies and practice have been slow to develop. Numerous opportunities now exist for more sensitive, safer intervention which places this issue firmly on the mainstream social work agenda.

Five Key Points

- Domestic violence is a problem relevant to all areas of social work practice, though frequently the issue is invisible or marginalized as other service priorities take precedence.
- Children are affected by witnessing violence and are more likely to be physically or sexually abused than children living in families where there is no domestic violence.
- The two key principles for effective work in this area include: developing interventions which direct responsibility towards the perpetrator (usually the man) and his abuse; working with domestic violence survivors (usually women and children) attending to their separate needs as well as recognizing that the child's safety will usually be linked to their mother's safety.
- Screening for domestic violence by asking sensitive questions will significantly increase awareness of the numbers of individuals using the agency who are affected by domestic violence.
- Domestic violence intervention requires effective collaboration in and between adult and children's services, as well as a wide range of other agencies including police, housing departments, and the courts.

Three Questions

? What issues affect women's decisions to stay in or return to a situation of domestic violence?

? What issues could be covered in risk assessment and safety planning with (i) women and (ii) children affected by domestic violence?

? What local services should be available to create more effective domestic violence intervention?

Further reading

1   Mullender, A., Kelly, L., Hague, G., Malos, E. and Iman, U. (2002) *Children's Perspectives on Domestic Violence*. London: Routledge.
2   Calder, M. (2005) *Children Living with Domestic Violence: Towards a Framework for Assessment and Intervention*. Lyme Regis: Russell House.
3   Humphreys, C. and Stanley, N. (eds.) (2006) *Domestic Violence and Child Protection: Directions for Good Practice*. London: Jessica Kingsley.

CHAPTER 2.1

Relating Theory to Practice

David Howe

In their day-to-day practice, social workers face a busy and complex world of human behaviour in a social context. It is a world in which relationships break down, emotions run high, and personal needs go unmet, a world in which some people have problems and some people are problems.

If they are to function in this confused mix of psychological upset and social concern, practitioners must begin to see pattern and order behind the tumult. They must try to understand and *make sense* of people and the situations in which they find themselves. Striving to make sense of experience is a fundamental characteristic of being human. If we are to cope with and be competent in social situations, we need to have ideas about what might be going on. This need becomes pressing in situations where need, stress and upset are present in large measure. Professionals who work in such situations develop more deliberate, systematic and formalized ways of making sense. It is these more self-conscious attempts to 'make sense' which we call 'theory'.

If social workers are to act clearly, competently and usefully in practical situations, they need to think theoretically. If we did not theorize, social life would remain a cauldron of unorganized experience and to all intents and purposes all practical action would be impossible. The join between theory and practice is a seamless one. And, it has often been said, there is nothing so practical as a good theory.

If practice is to be compassionate as well as appropriate, it is important that social workers retain a deep interest in people. The struggle to understand behaviour and relationships, actions and decisions, attitudes and motivations needs to be maintained at all times if practice is to be sensitive and effective. The more social workers think about, puzzle over and engage with people and the situations in which they find themselves, the more sense they will be able to make. The challenge is to remain curious about and thoroughly interested in people. The social worker needs constantly to ask herself the 'reason why' of things, to develop an active and enquiring mind. Why does this woman stay with her violent husband? Why is this four-year-old child so subdued and withdrawn? Why does this daughter feel so hostile towards her increasingly dependent 81-year-old mother? So, although there is no consensus about which theories best explain particular situations, there is agreement that practitioners who develop and offer coherent understandings of what might be going on are those best able to keep their professional bearings and sustain personal commitment. Both abilities are highly prized by the users of social work services.

The argument is that by analysing practice and reflecting on people's needs and relationships, social workers become clearer about their theoretical assumptions. However, it is also possible to turn this process around. As well as *induce* theory from practice and observation, it is also possible to *deduce* from theory what to do and what to see. The social worker in possession of a clear theoretical outlook finds that it guides and influences her practice in five key areas:

1   *Observation*: it tells her what to see and what to look out for.
2   *Description*: it provides a conceptual vocabulary and framework within which observations can be arranged and organized.
3   *Explanation*: it suggests how different observations might be linked and connected; it offers possible causal relationships between one event and another.
4   *Prediction*: it indicates what might happen next.
5   *Intervention*: it suggests things to do to bring about change.

Different theories, of course, lead to different observations and explanations. For example, in the case of a difficult toddler, the behaviourist notes that the young mother reinforces her child's poor behaviour by only giving him attention when he is naughty; the feminist practitioner is struck by the mother's stress, low self-worth and lack of support from her oppressive partner; and the social worker using a developmental perspective observes that the mother, who was neglected herself as a child, grows anxious and agitated when her son becomes too demanding and dependent. This is not to argue that these three observations are mutually exclusive. However, in practice it is often the case that a practitioner with a strong theoretical preference is inclined to observe, describe, explain, predict and intervene in a style and a language that is noticeably different from a social worker holding a contrasting theoretical outlook.

The Social Work Process

A simple but effective way of exploring the relationship between theory and practice is to ask a series of seemingly innocuous questions about a case or a piece of practice. By insisting on clear answers to these questions, the practitioner finds that she is able to reflect on matters at a surprisingly deep level. It is during this reflection process and the answer-giving stage that the relationship between theory and practice becomes explicit and available for discussion. Five questions can be asked of a case or piece of work:

1   *What is the matter?* This question helps the social worker define problems and identify needs. Supplementary questions might include: For whom is it a problem? Who benefits if the need is met?

2 *What is going on?* This is perhaps the most important question. It demands that the situation is assessed, analysed, diagnosed, interpreted or explained. The social worker makes sense of what is going on.

3 *What is to be done?* In the light of the assessment, goals are set, objectives identified, plans made and intentions declared.

4 *How is it to be done?* The methods, techniques, skills, services and resources needed to achieve the goals are chosen and deployed.

5 *Has it been done?* The outcome is reviewed and evaluated.

Different theories sponsor different answers to these five questions. But whatever the response, the answers and activities map out the basic features of the *social work process* with its five-stage sequence of: (1) the formulation of problems and the identification of needs, (2) the analysis of cases and the making of an assessment, (3) the setting of goals and objectives, (4) the design of methods of work and intervention, and (5) the review and evaluation of the involvement. This process describes a sequence and a structure to help social workers practise in a thoughtful and systematic way. It provides the basis of a disciplined and professional social work practice. It is also designed to overcome the tendency of social workers and their agencies to jump from problem to solution in one bound. Within the social work process, considerable importance is given to the stage of assessment. This is a time for reflection, enquiry and vigorous analysis. Assessments encourage practitioners to stop and think about what is going on. They provoke thought and liberate practice from the routine and humdrum.

Theories for Social Work

Things might be relatively simple and straightforward if social work was underpinned by one or two generally agreed theories for practice. In any one case the five questions of the social work process would receive a limited range of acceptable answers. Unfortunately, the theoretical world underpinning social work practice is a far from stable place. Because social workers deal with people in social situations, most of their theories, albeit adapted to the social work context, derive ultimately from psychology and sociology.

However, these primary disciplines have not established a consensus about the true character of human nature, individual development and social interaction. Although they strive to 'make sense' of people and society, the range of theories and understandings on offer are numerous and diverse. Sociology and psychology provide intellectual arenas in which fierce debates rage about the individual and society, the personal and the political, order and conflict, biology and culture, free will and determinism, causal explanation and subjective understanding. To the extent that social work's theories are based on psychological and sociological theories, they, too, will reflect the range, diversity and disagreements present in the parent disciplines.

So long as these epistemological disputes exist, there can be no universally agreed criteria by which to judge social work's theories and practices. This is not to say that some theories will not be preferred at certain times and in particular places.

11

Political and cultural factors also come into play and influence what is thought and what is done in the name of good social work. Nevertheless, social work theory remains a highly varied and contested activity. If the argument holds good that in practice there is no escape from theory, the social worker, denied an Archimedean point, needs to understand how and why different psychological and sociological theories vary as they do. Rather than bemoan the number and range of theories, the practitioner needs to acknowledge that the diversity reflects the subtlety and complexity of the human condition. Appreciation of the elegance and multi-dimensionality of these conceptual landscapes can be highly stimulating.

a classification of something resp. organisms

Types of Theory

Many frameworks and taxonomies have been developed to help practitioners find their way around social work's theories. The attempts to classify the theories rely on recognizing a limited range of key conceptual dimensions, various combinations of which help to define particular sets of related theories. At root, most of the classifications draw on discussions about human nature, the relative importance of biology, culture and experience in human development, and the social movements and ideological climates that define and shape human society (see Turner, 1996; Howe, 1987; Payne, 2005a). Mapping out social work's theoretical terrain helps practitioners locate themselves intellectually and invites them to explore new areas of thought and practice.

Although in some circles there is a coming together of psychology and sociology, these two disciplines still create one of the main divisions in social work theory between structural and psychological explanations of personal difficulty. Within the structural perspective, the focus is on the political, economic and material environment in which people find themselves. The approach includes anti-oppressive and anti-discriminatory perspectives. Poverty and inequality, the lack of opportunity and social injustice seriously disadvantage some people. The disadvantages induce stress, anxiety and 'poor social functioning'. Such problems bring them to the attention of society and its agents. However, structural theorists maintain that for these groups, the individual should not be seen as a problem for society, rather society should be seen as a problem for the individual. This outlook influences the way problems are defined, the type of assessment made, the goals planned and the social methods employed.

In practice, though, most social work theories remain heavily influenced by the more psychological approaches to human behaviour. There are many ways in which these psychological theories can be categorized. Most rely on making particular assumptions about human nature and the ways in which we learn, develop and respond. One simple division is to see whether a particular theory emphasizes either the client's emotional condition or his or her capacity for rational action.

Theories which pay most attention to the emotional side of people's lives and the quality of their relationships seek to understand present behaviour in terms of past experiences. The character of our relationship history influences our personality and social competence. As most social work clients experience or express difficulty in

[margin note: isa hypothetical vantage point from which an observer can objectively perceive the subject of inquiry with a view of totality.]

one or more of their key relationships (with partners, parents or children), it seems appropriate to try and understand the quality of their social and interpersonal development and how it might be affecting current behaviour. Understanding, support, nurturing, the meeting of emotional and developmental needs, containment and insight are present in many of the practices associated with these theories. By understanding past events, the client and the worker might be able to contain or make sense of current experiences. Making sense allows people to gain control of the meaning of their own experience and move into the future with a more robust, mature, independent and strengthened personality. Such a personality is likely to be more socially competent, and socially competent people handle relationships more effectively. Altering the meaning of experience brings about changes in behaviour.

Theories of this persuasion include all those which take a developmental perspective. They are person-focused. They consider people from the psychological inside. Psychoanalytic theory, attachment theory, theories of loss and separation, many forms of feminist theory and elements of the person-centred approach can all be placed within this broad category of developmentally orientated and relationship-sensitive approaches to social work practice.

Theories which appeal to clients' rational capacities and cognitive strengths tend to adopt a problem-solving approach. These approaches are based on the belief that people with problems can resolve them by the use of rational thought, cognitive understanding and behavioural advice. Practitioners work with clients in problem-solving partnerships. Typically, the approach involves:

- the identification, description and quantification of the problem;
- analysis of the factors, including the behaviour of other people, which maintain the problem;
- the selection of goals;
- the identification and implementation of those actions which will achieve the goals and resolve the problem.

Based on an analysis of present conditions, problem-solving approaches encourage clients to identify what steps they will need to take if they wish to move themselves into a problem-free future. Practice is often pragmatic, time limited and task-centred. People are viewed from the behavioural outside. The belief is that by changing behaviour, personal experience is improved.

 Social work theories that fall into this category include task-centred approaches, cognitive-behavioural theories, many forms of family therapy, brief solution-focused therapy and some aspects of systems theory.

Theory and Practice in Social Context

One further layer of analysis has to be added if we are to gain a full understanding of the relationship between social work theory and practice. Social work takes place and is formed within a social and political context. It occupies and is defined by the space between the personal and the political in which the state relates to the individual and the individual relates to the state. So, although social work practices need the help of the psychological and sociological sciences if they are to make sense of people in social difficulty, the *purposes* of social work and its practices are defined by a different set of intellectual traditions.

In the broadest sense, the purposes of social work are determined by prevailing political values. These values influence welfare legislation, political policy, government guidelines, and the distribution and definition of resources. The politically defined purposes of social work also influence the psychological and sociological theories chosen by practitioners to help them 'make sense' and practise.

Political philosophies which emphasize collective responsibility and action also value harmony and cooperation, equality and interdependence. They support theories and practices which are more structural, developmental and therapeutic in their outlook. Psychologically healthy development occurs only if the individual is embedded in a good quality social environment. A sense of belonging and being wanted in a community of close personal relationships is essential if a secure and coherent personality is to form.

A case example

Anna is aged 10. She lives with her mother and two younger brothers, aged 5 and 3 years. Anna's mother suffers depression. The family live in a large apartment block in a very disadvantaged part of the city. The school authorities have expressed concern about Anna's increasingly poor school attendance record.

Think of as many reasons as you can that might explain Anna's school attendance problem. What is the theoretical basis of each explanation?

When the political pendulum shifts away from welfare collectivism towards neo-liberal concepts of freedom, choice and personal responsibility in the context of a market economy, theories and practices tend towards the brief and the behavioural (Howe, 1996). The individual is seen as independent and free, disembedded from and unconstrained (and not limited) by his or her social environment. Such freedom and autonomy allows full scope for creative endeavour and the rational pursuit of what is in one's own best interests. Morally and psychologically, the individual must stand alone. Individuals are personally responsible for who they are and what they become, for what they do and how they do it. This represents a shift away from explaining people's psychological insides to measuring their behavioural outsides. The external performance, of both worker and client, becomes the unit of audit. *What* people do is more important than *why* they do it. Economic and political partnerships replace therapeutic relationships. The theories which come to the fore in this political climate are those which encourage brief, task-centred and behaviourally measurable practices in which the act rather than the actor becomes the focus of interest.

Summary

Practice, as defined by the social work process, varies as practitioners make use of different theories. Theories vary as they appeal to different understandings of human nature, personal development and society. And different theories come in and out of fashion as political values and social philosophies change with the flow of large social movements through history. Just as theory relates to practice, so practice relates to theory. Only the faint-hearted despair at the inordinate subtlety of personal experience and social life. So long as social workers retain a passionate interest in and concern for the quality of human experience, and so long as they strive to 'make sense', the relationship between theory and practice will continue to invigorate, fascinate and professionally uplift.

Five Key Points

- Social work theories help practitioners make sense of complex and difficult human situations.
- Different social work theories generate different understandings of human behaviour and social situations.
- The social work process of 'defining problems and needs – making an assessment – setting goals – carrying out methods to achieve those goals', describes a sequence and a structure which helps social workers practise in a systematic way.
- Social workers who use theory to inform their use of the social work process are more likely to practise in a thoughtful and professional manner.
- The purposes of social work and the theories which support them vary depending on the cultural context in which social work finds itself.

Three Questions

? How might different social work theories explain or make sense of the same case or social situation?
? What assumptions does a particular social work theory make about (a) human nature; (b) the influence of human biology, culture and social experience on personal development; and (c) appropriate political and personal values?
? In particular cases and situations, how do different social work theories influence the content of the social work process?

Further reading

1 Payne, M. (2005a) *Modern Social Work Theory*, 3rd edn. Basingstoke: Palgrave Macmillan.
2 Beckett, C. (2006) *Essential Theory for Social Work Practice*. London: Sage.
3 Coulshed, V. and Orme, J. (2006) *Social Work Practice: An Introduction*, 4th edn. Basingstoke: Palgrave Macmillan.

CHAPTER 4.4

Culture, Ethnicity and Identity

Kwame Owusu-Bempah

Due to Western nations' plundering and exploitation of the rest of the world, now euphemistically termed 'globalization', coupled with the USA's unrelenting quest for global dominance (Chomsky, 2004), modern migratory patterns have ensured that every culture, with its language, artefacts and practices, is represented in the UK, as elsewhere. Professional practice in today's multi-cultural, multi-ethnic and multi-faith world must, therefore, reflect this diversity. This chapter examines the influence of beliefs and assumptions about culture, ethnicity and identity on professional practice with black clients. The emphasis is on children and families.

Culture and Ethnicity

A generally accepted definition of culture is that it is a composite structure of the real and the symbolic: beliefs, mythology, religion, ideas, sentiments, institutions and objects of a given group transmitted generationally and internalized in varying degrees by its members. It includes child-rearing practices, kinship patterns and the ethics governing interpersonal relationships. It includes also ideas about person-hood: personal identity and group identity.

Although both *culture* and *ethnicity* are frequently used synonymously, there is a conceptual distinction between the two, as the following definitions of *ethnicity* illustrate:

> one of a number of [human] populations ... which individually maintain their differences ... by means of isolating mechanisms such as geographic and social barriers ... an ethnic group may be a nation, a people, a language or a [religion]. (Montagu, 1997, p. 186)

> a distinct category of the population in a larger society whose culture is usually different from its own ... the members of such a group are, or feel themselves, or are thought to be bound together by common ties of race or nationality or culture. (Morris, 1968, p. 167)

These definitions indicate that there is no single criterion by which *ethnic group* can be defined. They show also that everyone has multiple ethnicity in terms of geographical region, religion, social class, and so forth. Notwithstanding, ethnicity and culture are frequently used by professionals, politicians, the mass media and even the academic community not only interchangeably, but also to connote, and often denote, 'race', 'immigrant' or 'otherness'.

Self-identity

We derive our self-concept from our culture. In Western European cultures, children are socialized to see themselves as autonomous, free from all external control. The child is taught not only to possess mastery of him/herself, but also of everyone and everything, including even time. This conception of the self is alien to most cultures outside the West. Other cultures emphasize interdependence, and so prepare their children for reciprocal relationships in adulthood with the social, physical and spiritual worlds (Wiredu, 1998).

Various investigators inform us that, within the context of world cultures, an actualized person is one who is most deeply connected to others and society as a whole. For example, there are Pacific Island groups who view themselves not as bounded, distinct entities, but as integral pieces of an eternal life scheme (Lesser, 1996); there are Indian cultures where the deep inner self, upon maturity, is not seen as achieving unbridled autonomy, but as merging with the social and spiritual worlds (Roland, 1988); there are African cultures where one is less than human without 'Us', or where the individual seeks the answer to the question 'Who am I?' not only in the question 'Who are we?' but also in the question 'Who were we?' (Owusu-Bempah and Howitt, 2000). In the extreme, there is the Innu (Eskimo) culture that does not even have a word for self-reference (Page and Berkow, 1991). In other words, every culture is a different world with its own idiosyncrasies; meaning that there are as many conceptions of the self as there are cultures. The implications of this for professional interventions which claim to enhance the self-esteem of ethnic minority children in British society, children of diverse and radically different cultural, ethnic and social backgrounds to the therapist's, are clear. It also renders such social work rhetoric as 'black culture' or 'black perspective' nonsensical.

Culture, Ethnicity and Identity: An Interplay

Foster (1998) poses a number of questions to illustrate the fatuity of any attempt to generalize Western theoretical assumptions about culture, ethnicity, identity and psychotherapy. This is one such question:

> How do we figure out the deep self-experience of a Middle Eastern man from a religious sect, who feels that without the tribe he was trained to lead, his self-esteem is unformed, non-existent? Do we view this client through the American self-psychological terms of a narcissistically derailed self, through the Ego Psychology lens of a poorly differenti-ated self? Or rather, as a person centred in the ensembled self-experience of his Eastern

culture, where bonding to family and group kinship renders individuals who through-out life are deeply identified with others? (Foster, 1998, pp. 259–60)

Trying to face the hard clinical or practice-related questions posed by such clients forces us to re-examine our assumptions, theory and practice. A good start will be an acknowledgement that we can understand people only by respecting and studying how they understand themselves. People of every nationality, culture or ethnicity seek to understand themselves – their own character, their ways and peculiarities that differentiate them from other peoples.

It is ironic that despite the emphasis on ethnic and cultural restitution as a solution to the structural difficulties facing ethnic minority children in Britain, what passes for and is recommended as culture might best be described as a pastiche of a culture. Perhaps this is unsurprising given the miscomprehension about the nature of culture and ethnicity amongst practitioners. The simple truth is that the culture which practitioners see as a lifeline for their black and ethnic minority children has little or nothing to do with any indigenous culture. These interventions implicitly assume a monolithic culture for ethnic minority groups in British society. This is far from the truth.

Self-identity and Practice with Ethnic Minority Children

Practitioners very often conflate personal, 'racial', cultural and ethnic identities. This is quite apparent in social work where the issue concerning these terms has been hotly contested in recent years. The literature in the area of fostering/adoption is replete with claims that black children in the public care system as well as those fostered or adopted by white families experience more psychosocial developmental problems than other children, including their white counterparts. These problems are routinely ascribed to the children's lack of awareness of their 'black culture' (e.g. Small, 1991). For obvious reasons, this explanation, rather than racism, is favoured by the Children Act.

Although institutional racism is a more plausible explanation for the children's psychosocial developmental difficulties, the accepted solution is to 'work on' the children's self-identity. Many casually accept this practice. Others even advocate it as a necessary anti-racist strategy for social work with black adults as well. Some social services departments have taken these damaging assumptions seriously and have established special clinics to 'repair the damaged self-identity' of black children in their care. Briefly, social work and educational establishments increasingly refer black children to therapists to improve their racial identity or self-concept. Coward and Dattani (1993) drew attention to how child protection case conferences and statutory child care reviews routinely result in requests for professional involvement to improve black youngsters' self-image. Mullender (1991) also described a project designed to improve their self-confidence ostensibly because they are confused about their 'racial identity' as a consequence of being adopted or fostered by white families. Such an approach ignores obvious alternative causal factors, for example separation and loss (Owusu-Bempah, 2006), and attributes the youngsters' difficulties to their colour.

Unsurprisingly, programmes used to achieve this are ethnicity- or culture-based. They include providing the children with information about their 'black cultural background', including information about black historical figures and/or counselling them to identify with 'the black community' and to take pride in their 'blackness' (e.g. Banks, 1992; Maximé, 1994). Such programmes are guilty of victim-blaming (Owusu-Bempah, 1994). Conventionally, biological factors have been evoked to justify the plight of black people. Today psychological (self-identity) and social anthropological factors (culture/ethnicity) provide the excuse. It is no comfort to the children whatever is adduced to justify their difficulties if it remains at the level of the individual (the child or the family) and fails to tackle the structural barriers facing them in the larger society; it matters not a hoot the skin-colour of its proponents, or their intentions.

The programmes assume also that the children experience 'identity-crises' because they have favourable attitudes to the white community. For example, Maximé (1991, p. 103) described a 10-year-old black girl as psychologically disturbed, simply because she preferred 'a white family placement as black ones were all too poor'. Describing this girl's choice as astute, based upon reality, would be more meaningful. However, because of its policy and resource implications, such an interpretation would not be welcome. It would also seriously implicate black practitioners; it would challenge them to work toward dismantling the structural barriers which preclude black communities from providing homes and support to their young members who need such help and support, instead of colluding with the system by rationing and administering palliative measures to these children, including psychotherapy. As such, one must be forgiven for suspecting an (unwitting) coalition of conspiracy or interests (Owusu-Bempah, 2003).

As the above case (Maximé, 1991) shows, the programmes also equate 'non-affiliation' with one's ethnic group with psychological damage warranting intervention. It may be rather helpful to regard such behaviour as an example of 'negative identification'. Erikson (1968) saw negative identification as neither always nor necessarily harmful; and so must not be interfered with unnecessarily. Furthermore, it suggests that the identity crises (personal, ethnic or cultural) which black children are presumed to experience may be caused by adults' (notably social workers' and therapists') preconceptions and over-reaction to their exploration of aspects of different cultures to their own. This type of exploration or experimentation must be seen as a normal developmental process, given the variety of ways of life they are exposed to, as a result of growing up in a 'global village'.

Because 'race', culture and ethnicity are endemic in these programmes they confuse self-identity with ethnic/cultural identity. There is a distinction between the two concepts.

- Self-identity refers to an individual's sense of uniqueness, a unique personal property – what sets person A apart from person B; although a culture is shared by all its members, each member experiences it in a unique way, resulting in individual personalities.
- Ethnic or cultural identity relates to group identity, a 'racial', ethnic, cultural or social reference-group.

Owing to the confusion surrounding these concepts, ethnic minority groups are often presented as culturally homogenous, belonging to a single, monolithic culture shared by all ethnic minorities, regardless of their national or geographical origins. This illusory posture is likely to diminish the efficacy of programmes and practices in meeting clients' individual needs, or even harm them. Social workers' handling of Victoria Climbié's case is a crystalline example (Owusu-Bempah, 2003).

Negating the Other's Self-definition

The offspring of black and white unions are particularly singled out for pathologizing by helping professionals. The popular belief that identity crises are endemic to children of black and white unions is obviously no more than a racist assumption (Owusu-Bempah, 1994, 2005; Owusu-Bempah and Howitt, 1999). It is the ghost of the 'marginal man' evoked to haunt these children, to justify our unfair treatment of them. The notion of the 'marginal man' holds that they owe their marginal status in a racist society, and its concomitant social, economic and psychological disadvantages, to their inability to integrate their 'racial', ethnic and cultural identities. In modern British society, it is claimed that their psychological salvation lies only in identifying with the so-called black community (Maximé, 1994; Small, 1991). Is this not a reification of the 'one drop rule'? (Owusu-Bempah, 2005)

Systematic activities to deal with this putative psychological disturbance involve, explicitly or implicitly, denying their white side, a process which many of the children find emotionally painful, damaging and undesirable (Tizard and Phoenix, 1993/2002). The underlying assumption is equally paralogistical, as well as bizarre: if it is acceptable for these children to identify with their black side, what is problematic about their identification with their white side? Who should decide which aspects of their heritage should be significant to them, the children or those who want them to see themselves as 'black'? Briefly, which 'racial', ethnic or cultural side of their inheritance they feel comfortable with is largely determined by their own experiences and the subjective meanings of those experiences to them; denial of the 'black' label, or group-rejection, is not necessarily symptomatic of a personality disturbance. Numerous empirical studies using a wide variety of procedures over the last several decades support this view (e.g. Cross, 1991; Wilson, 1987). It is an irony that those professionals who try to foreclose these children's identity at the same time claim to subscribe to human diversity, ethnic and cultural diversity.

Allen (1997) argues that identity, like 'race', ethnicity/culture, continues to loom large in the practitioner–ethnic-minority-client relationship, to the virtual exclusion of structural factors because:

> The [Western] concept of the self as a separate, atomistic, private, autonomous individual has been constituted by specific, complex, social, economic, historical, cultural and psychological relations .. not only is [it] philosophically inadequate, but also serves neo-colonial and imperial goals of domination. (Allen, 1997, p. 9)

Bhavnani (1994) agrees with this view in describing the concept of intelligence as a psychological tool of subjugation, domination and control. In social work, as in other social institutions, 'race'/ethnicity has historically served this purpose. It is now unacceptable to espouse overt racist theories to justify the provision of second-class services to ethnic minority clients. Invoking 'black inferiority' under the guise of ethnicity, culture or identity serves this purpose safely. It does so more expediently and effectively because, as the literature reveals, it has the support and cooperation of ethnic minority professionals, particularly social workers, teachers and therapists.

Black Culture, Black Perspectives

What social work model is needed to provide appropriate services to diverse populations? One common way of dealing with this is to highlight practitioners' poor knowledge and understanding of the cultures of ethnic minority clients. This offers the expedient solution of establishing units of ethnic minority 'experts' to service ethnic minority communities; black-on-black practice is an obvious example (Owusu-Bempah, 2003). Apart from holding ethnic minority workers responsible for solutions to the structural problems facing ethnic minority clients, it is deskilling. Owing to modern migratory patterns, the population of the UK (like that of any nation) comprises numerous ethnic and cultural groupings. The excessive demands (implicit in the Children Act) that would be placed on any practitioner wishing to be competent to know something of the cultures of all sectors of society can be illustrated, for example, by briefly examining language – one of the key elements of any culture. Knappert (1995) estimates that over a thousand different languages (discounting dialects) are spoken in Africa alone. No practitioner could be expected to understand even the beliefs and practices relating to health, illness and psychological functioning of so many different cultures. It is, therefore, not surprising that issues of race, culture and ethnicity often cause anxiety both in everyday social exchanges and in the activities of practitioners.

Is cultural or ethnic/colour match a solution to the difficulty? Although a practitioner may be knowledgeable about a particular culture or language, factors such as social class and status differential may also militate against professional effectiveness. The use of ethnic/cultural match does not automatically ensure effective outcomes. We saw the dire consequence of this in Victoria Climbé's case. The practitioners' professional background and training, based on Western values and assumptions, such as those regarding the 'normal' individual or 'healthy' family, may offset any gains from ethnic/colour match (see Owusu-Bempah, 2003). Furthermore, the sharing of ethnicity by professionals and their clients does not always exclude the intrusion of stereotypes. Hall (1997, p. 645) argues that 'not all the perpetrators of cultural errors are white'. Again, this reminds us of the cultural misjudgement by Climbié's key social worker.

Of course, there are training models designed to prepare practitioners for effective work with ethnic minority clients. Characteristically, however, such training has been dominated by issues of 'race', ethnicity and culture (and 'political correctness'). It must be stressed that this can easily lead to feelings of insecurity amongst practitioners whose sense of a lack of competence in matters of ethnicity and culture can make them feel deskilled; it may also serve as an excuse for professional inertia.

21

This emerged in the Victoria Climbié Inquiry (Laming, 2003). Additionally, training programmes and practices which over-emphasize ethnic/cultural issues can be criticized for lacking a clear conceptual framework or for trying to use simplistic and formulaic methods to solve complex structural problems. Cacas (1984, p. 465) called such models and practices 'cultural *generalizations*, when the practitioner assumes that all presenting problems are related to the client's culture/ethnicity rather than to other factors'.

Conclusion: Closing Gaps

The UN Convention on the Rights of the Child emphasizes that the goal of child care practice should be to achieve equality for *all* children, whoever, whatever and wherever they may be; that it should aim at closing social, educational and economic gaps; an important goal of child care practice must be to reduce social inequalities; the removal of discriminations, especially normative discriminations which are covertly institutionalized. Ascribing ethnic minority children and their families' difficulties to their colour, ethnicity, culture or psychological functioning, and dealing with them through psychological means is an admission of institutional racism, of 'racial' inequality in society.

The focus of social services departments has been on describing and explaining ethnic-minority-service-users' 'pathology'. Pollard (1989) has suggested an 'empowering' two-pronged approach to work with ethnic minority children and families, and other disadvantaged families. The approach distinguishes between 'alterable' and 'static' variables. 'Alterable variables' relate to factors in a person or the environment which can be manipulated somehow to enhance their functioning. 'Static variables' represent factors that are not easily changed, but only classify or label people; ethnicity, culture and self-identity are examples. In the case of children in care, for example, the 'alterable variables' approach seeks to:

- identify those children who seem to be thriving in the system and determine what factors are associated with their resilience;
- identify those factors within the system or environment which deleteriously affect, as well as those which enhance, their functioning.

This framework requires a positive attitude towards ethnic minority families, such as identifying, fostering and encouraging their strengths. It is similar to Wakefield's (1996) eco-systems approach to the social work assessment process. Both approaches are different from the problem-family/client model which pathologizes even the strengths of these families, such as the extended family structure, and adoption/fostering within the community.

While it is unlikely that few practitioners would assume a monocausality to problems in black childhood, for instance, their failure to identify clearly what distinguishes a racial/ethnic or cultural identity problem from any other causes means that the boundaries are fuzzy and that culture, ethnicity or identity may be blamed unnecessarily. A preoccupation with skin tone, ethnicity/culture is likely to obscure the assessment process resulting in misinterpretations of ethnic minority clients' needs and the provision of inappropriate services to them.

Five Key Points

- Assumptions about 'race' culture, ethnicity and identity have a negative impact on service-provision for ethnic minorities in British society.
- British society is a complex web of cultures.
- Conceptually as well as in practice, 'black culture' is a nonentity.
- Providing effective services to diverse populations requires cultural competence more than cultural knowledge.
- Helping professionals face a formidable task in a world in constant flux.

Three Questions

? There is no empirical foundation to own-race adoption and fostering policies and practices. Discuss.

? What is the relationship between 'race', culture, ethnicity and self-identity?

? An important goal of social work must be to reduce social inequalities. Discuss with reference to ethnic minority clients.

Further reading

1 Owusu-Bempah, K. and Howitt, D. (2000) *Psychology beyond Western Perspectives.* Oxford: Blackwell.
2 O'Hagan, K. (2001). *Cultural Competence in the Caring Professions.* London: Jessica Kingsley.
3 Okitikpi, T. (ed.) (2005). *Working with Children of Mixed Parentage.* Lyme Regis: Russell House.

CHAPTER 4.5

Families

Graham Allan

Since the early days of industrialization, the decline of family life has regularly been lamented. Throughout this time, pleas to 'strengthen the family', to preserve 'family values' and to ensure that the next generation is properly socialized have been ever-present. Such moral and political rhetoric can undoubtedly be influential in shaping legislative action which directly affects the welfare of different families. For example, the state's actions in 'policing' and monitoring the behaviour of families through its various agencies, including social work, health visiting and other services, help to shape the boundaries of what constitutes acceptable family relationships. So too, regulations governing welfare benefits and tax advantages have a noticeable impact on family well-being. Yet claims made about the demise of family life have generally misrepresented the real character of the changes occurring. Not only has historical analysis demonstrated that contemporary family dilemmas – domestic violence, child abuse or family dissolution – are not new, but as importantly, families continue to be seen by those involved as arenas in which personal security and emotional satisfaction can be expected, if not always achieved.

Confusion often arises within popular discourses because change in family organization is frequently viewed as inherently negative. Romantic visions of the past are glorified, so that almost any change gets defined as damaging. Yet precisely because family relationships are both personally and socially significant, family organization cannot be expected to remain static. Any social institution which is central to the workings of a society is necessarily integrated with other key aspects of economic and social structure. Consequently, that institution must itself alter as these other aspects are modified under new social and economic conditions. In this regard, dominant family forms cannot remain constant and still be institutionally significant. They must change to reflect transformations in other spheres of social and economic activity. From a sociological angle, this is the key to understanding family life: family organization is inevitably patterned by the wider social and economic formation, even if ideologically the family is presented as being separate and apart – a cosy private domain located in an increasingly threatening public world.

Changing Families and Households

In Britain over the last thirty years, as elsewhere in the Western world, there have been radical changes in the demography of family life (Allan and Crow, 2001; Lewis, 2001b). While debate continues about whether these changes reflect a genuine reordering of family relationships – between parents and children, husbands and wives, and wider kin – three areas of change can be identified as particularly significant.

First, there have been major changes in patterns of coupledom and family formation. Aside from gay couples now being more accepted, the growth in cohabitation has been particularly remarkable. According to the data available, relatively few people cohabited outside of marriage until the early 1970s. The typical pattern was one of youthful marriage following a formal engagement which often involved elements of a sexual relationship but stopped well short of living together. Currently, cohabitation has not only become the dominant form of engagement in that most couples now do cohabit prior to marriage, but as importantly, increasing numbers of couples now cohabit whether or not they are planning to marry. For example, only 11 per cent of non-married women aged between 18 and 49 were cohabiting in 1979; by 2002, the figure was 29 per cent (General Household Survey, 2004). From being a stigmatized form of coupledom, cohabitation has become a normal phase, receiving social approval rather than opprobrium. Moreover as cohabitation has increased, it is now becoming evident that there has been a concomitant decline in marriage. This is not just an issue of later marriage but also one of people choosing not to marry at all. Officially it is estimated that by 2031 some 46 per cent of the adult male population and 39 per cent of the adult female population will never have married, compared to 35 per cent of adult men and 28 per cent of adult women in 2003 (Government Actuary's Department, 2005). The figures were far lower a generation or so ago when roughly 90 per cent of people married.

The second major change has been the growth in levels of partnership separation and divorce. While legislative change has clearly facilitated increased divorce, the

Table 1 *Selected family changes in England and Wales, 1971–2001*

	1971	*1986*	*2001*
Number of first marriages	320,347	220,372	148,642
Women's average age at first marriage	21.4	23.1	27.7
Number of second marriages	84,390	127,552	100,585
Rate of divorce per 1,000 marriages	5.9	12.9	13.0
Children under 16 of divorcing parents	82,304	151,964	146,914
Number of lone-parent families[a]	570,000	1,010,000	1,750,000[b]
Percentage of all births to unmarried mothers	9.2	21.4	40.0
Percentage of teenage births to unmarried mothers	25.8	68.9	89.4

[a] These figures are for Great Britain.
[b] This figure is for the year 2000.
Sources: http://www.statistics.gov.uk/ (Birth Statistics Series FM1; Marriage, Divorce and Adoption Statistics Series FM2); Haskey, (1998); Haskey, (2002).

root causes go far deeper, reflecting – and in turn encouraging – fundamental shifts in the ways people define a satisfactory and acceptable marriage. Over time, there has been considerable movement in what Cancian (1987) usefully terms 'marital blueprints'. These have developed to emphasize the expectation of intimacy and mutual fulfilment through the quality of the couple relationship itself. A failure in this regard within a relationship is increasingly recognized as grounds for reconsidering its future (Jamieson, 1998). The result is that some 40 per cent of those marrying this year will divorce – more if the divorce rate continues to increase as it has been doing. Moreover each year, some 150,000 children under the age of 16 experience their parents' divorce. In addition, increasing numbers of children whose parents cohabit are also experiencing parental separation without this being officially recorded. Debates continue about how children's interests can be best protected during the process of parental separation and divorce (Richards, 1999).

Third, there have been major changes in patterns of child-bearing. As well as women having children later, there is far less expectation that mothers should be married. In 1973, only 9 per cent of all mothers, and 28 per cent of teenage mothers, were unmarried. Thirty years later, these figures had risen to 41 per cent and 90 per cent respectively (Office of Population and Census Surveys, 1974; Office for National Statistics, 2004c). While some 63 per cent of unmarried mothers are cohabiting with their child's father at the time of the birth, this is by any standards a mammoth demographic shift in a single generation. It reflects the changed social vision about the place of marriage (and divorce) within society and altered images of what individuals, and especially women, should be striving for in constructing their personal lives. Together with increased levels of partnership separation and divorce, it has contributed to major increases in the number of lone-parent families.

Because of these and other associated changes in family patterns – including increased numbers of remarriages, repartnering and stepfamilies – new approaches to analysing family life have needed to be developed (Silva and Smart, 1999; Lewis, 2001b). In the past, social science discourses were often based around some notion of 'the normal family'. While the relationships, domestic roles and kinship responsibilities of these 'normal' families were not static, they were nonetheless characterized by what now seems a curious sense of uniformity. This was best captured by the notion of the family or domestic cycle through which families typically passed: marriage; child-bearing; child-rearing; the 'denuded' family once children had left home; and the death of one of the spouses. At the beginning of the twenty-first century, such images of 'normal' families have become increasingly problematic. What has emerged is a higher degree of diversity in family patterns and a greater variation in the pathways different families follow. This has repercussions for how 'normal' families are defined (Allan and Crow, 2001).

With increases in cohabitation, in childbirth outside marriage, in divorce, and in remarriage and stepfamily formation, there can be no assumed or standard familial pathway. Recognizing that these factors can affect people's experiences in both childhood and adulthood, it is evident that over the course of their lives different people follow quite distinct family pathways. So it is reasonable to talk of 'family course' or 'family pathway' but it is not sensible to think in terms of structured, patterned family careers that are common for the majority of people in the way that the notion of 'family cycle' implies. Yet in recognizing this, it is important to be aware that different pathways have implications for the family issues and problems which people face and which influence family decisions. There is no suggestion of randomness in this; family life may not follow a tidy schema, but earlier household and family structures still impact on later experiences.

Because 'the family' appears at nearly all times to be seen as under threat and in need of protection and strengthening, many of the issues which have rightly concerned social workers should be recognized as matters which indicate less a fall in public and private standards and more the emergence of new discourses and practices about the ways family relationships should be ordered (Morgan, 2004). In analysing the emergence of these 'problems', it becomes apparent that demographic change and family organization are only part of the process. What also matters is the interplay of moral, political and professional responses to the difficulties families of different forms face.

Many of the 'family problems' with which social workers have to grapple – child abuse, marital breakdown, domestic violence, family support for elderly people – are discussed elsewhere in this book, so will not be considered here. Instead the focus is on one particular 'issue': the growth of lone-parent families and the development of different understandings of these families. Examining the 'social construction' of lone-parent families illustrates some of the means by which aspects of family life become problematized within public discourses and highlights the dangers of too readily generalizing about the consequences of particular family and household structures.

Lone-parent Families

The numbers of lone-parent families have increased substantially from 0.6 million in 1971 to nearly 1.8 million in 2000. In 1971 there were approximately one million dependent children in lone-parent families, but by 2000 this had increased to 2.9 million (Haskey, 2002). It is probable that these trends will continue for some time. This represents more than a quarter of all households with dependent children living in them, compared to 8 per cent in 1971 (General Household Survey, 2004). Of course, these figures are 'snap-shots': they represent the number of adults and children in lone-parent families at a given time. Others will have experienced living in lone-parent families, but now be independent or part of stepfamilies through cohabitation or (re-)marriage.

Just as family life in general has become more diverse, so the experiences of lone-parent families are also varied (Rowlingson and McKay, 2002). Many factors influence the circumstances in which they operate. However, the single most common characteristic of such families remains poverty; despite significant changes in policy, material disadvantage is the norm. Only a minority of lone-parent families has sufficient resources to manage comfortably. In particular, female-headed lone-parent families, which comprise 90 per cent of all such families, are especially likely to be experiencing financial hardship. In 2002 Bradshaw reported that nearly three-fifths of all children in lone-parent families were living in poverty (Bradshaw, 2002, p. 135), with children in these families comprising half of all children in poverty (see also Rowlingson and McKay, 2002). The reasons for this include the low level of women's earnings, especially for those women with few qualifications; the pattern of mothers in Britain re-entering the labour force in a part-time capacity; and the difficulties of securing adequate child-care provision, despite important policy initiatives since the late 1990s. Thus even though there has been an increase since 1997 in the number of lone parents in employment – 56 per cent in 2005 – this employment is often low paid and insecure. Moreover in 2005, there were 1.2 million children living with lone parents where the parent was not in employment, the vast majority of whom were dependent on benefits (Department of Work and Pensions, 2005; Evans et al., 2004).

Lone-parent families tend also to be disadvantaged in terms of housing. One indicator of this is the disproportionate number living in rented accommodation rather than owner-occupation. In 2002, nearly two-thirds of lone-parent families lived in rented housing compared to less than a quarter of other families (General Household Survey, 2004). Similarly, lone-parent families are three times as likely as other families to be living in flats rather than houses (22 per cent and 7 per cent respectively). They are also generally likely to have less space and fewer household amenities than do two-parent families. Moreover many of those with least resources live in more run-down urban areas with poorer schooling, health care and other services (Rowlingson and McKay, 2005).

Social concern for lone-parent families has a long history, much of it less than progressive. The welfare of children in such families is a recurring theme, but so too is the burden of support which the state bears. In the mid-twentieth century, welfare measures aimed at increasing social participation and citizenship rights, including the development of health, education and income support services, covered lone-parent families just as much as any other family and household forms. However, there was at this time a sense in which lone-parent families were seen as pathological and in need of extra support. A metaphorical red light flashed in the minds of social welfare professionals in their dealings with lone-parent families, warning them that special provision might be necessary.

As the number of lone-parent families increased, this potentially stigmatizing professional benevolence became less marked. The red light no longer flashed, certainly not as brightly. Instead there was greater acceptance of the 'normality' of lone-parent families and a recognition that many of their problems were caused by poverty rather than family disorganization or personality disorders. Yet concern with reducing state expenditure since the 1980s has led to the 'problem' of lone-parent families being redefined. The high dependence of lone mothers on state benefits and state housing, the increasing numbers of divorces and births to single mothers, and the apparent failure of non-married fathers to accept financial responsibility for their children resulted in the state seeking ways to limit its commitments. Policies have been developed, especially since 1997, to encourage more lone mothers to find employment and greater pressure has been placed on non-residential fathers to make adequate financial contributions to their children's needs. The Child Support Agency was created in 1993 to police this and enforce compliance by aberrant fathers, in an effort to reduce the costs which the state bore in providing financial support to lone-parent families.

By the beginning of the twenty-first century, continuing concerns over social exclusion and inadequate socialization had 'politicized' lone-parent family issues further. For a period in the mid-1990s, the idea of 'underclass' captured popular concerns about the interplay between individual pathology and social divisions. Although the underclass was not restricted to lone-parent families, some, in particular young unmarried mothers and those who had been dependent on state support long-term, were certainly seen as core to it. Like earlier notions of 'cultures of poverty' and 'cycles of deprivation', the concept of 'underclass' highlighted the idea that children lacking the benefits of a 'normal' family environment come to be socialized into dysfunctional patterns of behaviour and hold sub-cultural values at odds with those of the mainstream. These discrepant values and behavioural patterns, instilled into the next generation thereby supposedly perpetuating the underclass, are then seen as a principal cause of poverty. While such views – not least the idea of lone mothers rejecting values associated with the material and other benefits of coupledom – have been heavily criticized in academic research, the main issue concerns the ways in which public visions of particular family forms and particular family problems are modified within a changing socio-political climate.

The emphasis on 'social exclusion' introduced by New Labour governments since 1997 focuses more on structural issues and personalizes social disadvantage rather less. Moreover, with the continuing demographic changes there have been in family life, lone-parent families are now culturally accepted more as a variant rather than deviant family form. Yet a tension nonetheless remains, especially with regard to those lone-parent families headed by young mothers with fewest resources. These mothers are often still portrayed as feckless and irresponsible, and as playing a 'welfare state' game for the housing and other material benefits they can accrue. Yet it is evident that these families experience significant hardship, constantly struggling to manage on inadequate resources. This has clear consequences for the well-being of both the women and children involved. Not only are they effectively excluded from many of the activities defined as socially normative, they are also disadvantaged in a range of other ways which exacerbate their more immediate problems of coping with economic deprivation. For example, the correlation between poverty and poor health is firmly established, as is the link between educational under-achievement and deprived material background. It is not surprising then that these families are likely to be defined as 'problem families' and to require disproportionate amounts of support from health and welfare agencies.

Conclusion

As the social and economic basis of society alters so too does the structure and organization of domestic and reproductive relations. With the increasing separation of sex, marriage and child-rearing, the complexity of family relationships has undoubtedly increased. This in turn is reflected in popular imagery and language about family patterns. New ideas evolve about what is appropriate for families and what is problematic. However, not all the new complexities of family life attract the same public concern. While some lone-parent families have continued to be problematized, other family matters which generate equal levels of personal concern and potentially have an impact on children's development are left largely outside public action.

Consider particularly the increasing number of stepfamilies. Research has pointed to the complex dynamics inherent in these families. Certainly for children the advent of a new 'parent' can raise all manner of emotional tensions, resentment and ambiguity. To develop successfully, these relationships require considerable investment and understanding. Yet the state apparently regards the formation of stepfamilies as unproblematic, if anything viewing them as 'solutions' to the problems of divorce and lone-parenthood. Thus there are relatively few official services provided for people entering stepfamilies, even at the level of protecting the interests of children. These families are defined as 'normal' and as quite capable of meeting their own needs without additional support. In many respects the 'problem families' continue to be defined as those in poverty who rely on state welfare benefits and public housing. Caught in a vortex of material disadvantage, there is an ever-present tendency to redefine their problems in terms of their own personal inadequacies, despite all that is known about the difficulties of sustaining family well-being with inadequate resources.

Five Key Points

- In recent years the diversity of family life has increased.
- There have been radical shifts in patterns of family formation and dissolution.
- Changes in family and domestic relationships need to be understood in the context of other social and economic changes.
- Poverty continues to be a common experience for the increasing numbers of lone-parent families.
- Economic and political factors influence the processes through which 'families with problems' become defined as 'problem families'.

Three Questions

? How can the processes of divorce and stepfamily formation be best managed from the viewpoint of children?
? What role does state action, including the activities of social welfare professionals, play in shaping domestic life?
? What impact has the decline of marriage had on social work practice?

Further reading

1   Allan, G. and Crow, G. (2001) *Families, Households and Society*. Basingstoke: Palgrave.
2   Lewis, J. (2001) *The End of Marriage? Individualism and Intimate Relations*. Cheltenham: Edward Elgar.
3   Rowlingson, K. and McKay, S. (2002) *Lone-Parent Families: Gender, Class and State*. Harlow: Prentice Hall.

CHAPTER 4.6

Sexuality and Sexual Relationships

Siobhan Canavan and Seamus Prior

Sexuality issues in social work practice are legion. We may quickly identify a wide range of areas of social work practice where sexuality issues arise. For example:

- the loss of intimacy for an older person who loses a partner either because of bereavement or admission to residential care;
- the sexuality of vulnerable adults living in the community;
- the sexual abuse of vulnerable adults in residential settings;
- sexual behaviour between children and young people;
- inappropriate sexual behaviour of some people with dementia;
- the sexuality of social workers and the impact of this on their practice;
- the exposure of children to parental sexual behaviour;
- the sexual abuse of children by trusted adults, including care workers;
- the housing of sex offenders in local communities;
- the placing of adults in mixed sex wards or care establishments at a time of psychological or physical vulnerability.

Sexuality presents one of the most complex and emotive areas in which social work professionals are required to make assessments and decisions. The general proliferation of sexual expressiveness in the media has not necessarily been matched by an increased individual capacity to reflect on and discuss sexual thoughts, feelings and behaviours. Although issues relating to sexuality are rarely the main reason for people coming into contact with social work agencies, they are often inherent and implicit in direct practice with service users. While sexuality issues evoke taboos and provoke anxiety, service users require of their social workers the facility to engage in the contemplation and discussion of sexual issues both to promote the service user's healthy sexual development and to protect them and others from harm. Service users may look to their social workers to initiate conversations on sexuality and workers need to develop the requisite skills to engage in these issues without being intrusive or causing unnecessary anxiety. There are four main areas in which social workers need to be aware of issues relating to sexuality and sexual relationships: first, they have a role in supporting service users in their sexual choices and preferences; secondly, they have a statutory role in protecting vulnerable people from sexual exploitation; thirdly, they need to be aware of not making assumptions regarding sexuality or sexual activity; and fourthly, they are required to demonstrate cultural sensitivity in this terrain.

Recent years have seen the construction of a more comprehensive body of knowledge on topics relating to sexuality and related aspects of social work practice. This may be a consequence of better training, publicity relating to sexual exploitation and a more open society in which matters relating to sexuality are more widely debated. The worker's own sexuality is also significant, as is the organizational context in which social work practice is carried out. With a professional commitment to practice which addresses issues of power, difference and diversity and the requirement for a sound knowledge base for practice, the imperative for an individual worker to address issues relating to sexuality is considerable. Here, we offer an overview of some issues which might be considered when thinking about sexuality and social work practice, starting with a consideration of the complexities of the issue.

Defining the Territory

Sexuality is a significant part of our lives although we may want to debate the usefulness of assuming that there is a common set of ideas about sexuality when the concept is so differently expressed between cultures, from one person to another and at various points in history and in a person's life course. The emergence of social movements concerned with sex and sexuality – the gay movement in particular – have challenged ideas about sexual preference, identity and choice. Feminism too has exposed the multiple forms of domination of women in the sexual arena – sexual violence and harassment, the language of sexual denigration and abuse. It has also posed questions about reproductive rights, sexual desire and pleasure. In all of this we are challenged to rethink the nature of our understanding about sexuality and the interconnectedness of influences and forces that shape our emotions, needs, desires and relationships.

Irrespective of their sexual orientation, young people in their teenage years have common issues relating to being in relationships, making informed choices about choosing whether to become sexually active or not, and practising safer sex. Many young people feel coerced into sexual activity because of peer pressure and they will need support if they make different choices from their peers. Others may go through a process of questioning their sexual orientation. For example, young people who have difficulty in acknowledging a sexual orientation other than straight, may have behavioural problems which lead to them coming into care. If the young person has experienced same-sex feelings or relationships they will need sensitive work and support. They may experience victimization by other children, compounding an already fragile sexual identity. If staff have not looked at the issue in training they may believe that there is something wrong with being lesbian or gay and pathologize the young person rather than offer them the support which they need. Social workers need to recognize that many adolescents question their sexual orientation and may need support in this process. If a young person identifies as gay or lesbian, for example, they may need support if faced with family disapproval or rejection. They may also need help in developing a social network.

There are four different, but related themes which are helpful in locating sexuality and its relationship to sex and gender. First, there is its biological and physical base. It includes sexual arousal, the act of having sex, responding to sexual stimuli and fantasy and relating to other people. As such, the sexual response is physiological, located in the body's reactions. Secondly, there is the question of the function of sexual activity in any relationship, whether it is a casual encounter, a long-term partnership, consensual or not. Not only can it be a way of expressing intimacy, love and affection, it can also be used as a way of exerting power or inflicting pain. This takes us into the arena of sexual abuse and exploitation. Thirdly, there is the question of the way in which feelings are managed in sexual relationships. A knowledge of psychology and human relationships can help here, as can the knowledge about the effect of childhood experiences on adult sexual behaviour. Fourthly, there is a need for an understanding of the relationship between sexuality, power and gender.

Self-awareness, Sexuality and Gender

The confidence and competence with which social workers are able to address issues of sexuality are largely dependent on the extent to which they have worked on their own issues around sex, sexuality and sexual relationships. It is essential that they have an understanding of their own sexuality, no matter how confused or unsettled this feels. This means recognizing the extent to which their sexuality has been affected by their history and the personal significance of gender, class, faith beliefs, age and ethnicity. Understanding ourselves is vital to the process of understanding others and in the area of sexuality this has particular significance when social workers are called on by their clients to respond to a range of issues including sexual preference, sex education, sexual exploitation, sexual violence, problem pregnancies and choosing whether or not to be sexually active.

Sexuality issues cannot be understood or appreciated without reference to gender. The increasing public awareness of child sexual abuse perpetrated by male care workers has had the cumulative effect of inhibiting male social workers from addressing sexual issues which arise in their practice. Men may be concerned that raising sexual matters with managers or colleagues will be judged inappropriate or indicative of a sexual motive on their part. In direct work with service users, men are rightly cautious that references to sexuality may be misinterpreted by service users, especially those with a history of sexual abuse. Anxiety in relation to sexuality may leave male workers feeling professionally deskilled and personally vulnerable, especially when their work involves providing intimate personal care. At the same time there is an unquestioned assumption that women are comfortable with providing personal care for men. A failure to grapple with, and find a way through, this discomfort and anxiety may result in traditional gender roles being reinforced, leaving women with the burden of personal care and the responsibility for addressing issues relating to sexuality or the body, further perpetuating the anxiety that men are not to be trusted in these areas.

Workers need to be clear about how their personal value base in relation to sexual issues may converge with or diverge from ethical and responsible practice. For example, when it comes to light that a 15-year-old boy in care is accessing Internet pornography, the worker's own attitude to pornography may affect what is regarded as an appropriate professional response. A male social worker who uses pornography unquestioningly in his private life may minimize the potential harm of this activity to the young person, advocating for the young man's rights to privacy, autonomy and freedom of expression, based on an unarticulated assumption that pornography is both ubiquitous and a normal part of male adolescent sexual development. This worker may not be able to undertake the assessment required in this situation to gauge the nature, content, frequency and circumstances of the young person's use of pornography and its consequential impact on his thinking, feelings, attitudes and behaviour.

Social workers with strong faith beliefs which condemn homosexuality need to address how they can promote the healthy sexual development of their lesbian, gay, bisexual or transgender (LGBT) service users. From another perspective, social workers who are personally very committed to LGBT equality issues need to be cautious that they do not inadvertently encourage service users who are questioning their sexual orientation to 'come out' when they are not ready to do so, when they may be exploring the possibility of same-sex attraction rather than identifying themselves as LGBT.

Social work, Sexuality and Vulnerable Adults

While, previously, vulnerable adults were cared for in institutions, where sexual behaviour could be prevented or minimized through prohibition, punishment and supervision, or covered up in an organizational culture of denial and silence, community care has now placed the sexuality of vulnerable adults under the public and professional spotlight. Social workers face ethical and moral dilemmas in balancing an adult's right to freedom of sexual expression with their responsibility to protect vulnerable people from exploitation. These dilemmas are highlighted in the situation of a sexually active adult woman with a learning disability living in the community. While she may be content in what she regards as a fulfilling and consensual relationship, others may see her as being ruthlessly exploited for the sexual gratification of another. If this is a heterosexual relationship, there is the further complication of potential pregnancy, raising issues of the service user's right to parenthood, their parenting capacity and the protection of a child born into such a situation. These circumstances have led some social work departments to seek permission through the courts for sexually active women with learning disabilities to be forcibly sterilized. The rationale offered in defence of these actions is that it offers protection to the women from the trauma of pregnancy and the responsibilities of child-rearing and that it is an effective form of contraception. So here the granting of rights in two areas – integration into the community and the right to have intimate relationships – is paid for by the denial of rights to reproduce and to parent.

Sexuality and Young People

One of the most sensitive areas for children and family social workers is the assessment of sexual behaviour between children. Research has shown that children and young people are as likely to be abused by other young people as by adults, calling into question the common assumption that sexual behaviour among young people may be regarded as playful or developmentally appropriate, a normal part of growing up (Cawson et al., 2000). Social workers need to be able to distinguish between sexual behaviour which is mutually consenting, exploratory and age-appropriate and that which is coercive, exploitative and abusive. Key to such assessment is the capacity to discuss sexual behaviour and feelings with children, young people, their parents and carers, and to evaluate the subjective meanings which young people attribute to sexual incidents in which they are involved. Assessment and intervention need to balance the rights of the young person to privacy and freedom of sexual expression and the responsibility invested in social workers to protect children from harm. Young people also need to learn to be responsible in their sexual behaviour and to know that they have the right to choose not to be sexually active, when peer and media pressure make this difficult.

The complexity of this area is seen in the provision of residential care where young women who may be accommodated on account of their vulnerability to sexual exploitation are placed in settings with young men who may pose a significant risk to them. A natural tendency to regard young people in the care system as casualties of troubled family histories may result in professional reluctance to make a realistic assessment of the risks that they might pose to other vulnerable young people. Workers may be torn between the desire to protect young people from the further stigmatization that the label 'a potential risk to others' might impose and their duty to ensure that others are adequately protected. This dilemma, reflected in the ongoing care versus control debate, may be acute in relation to young people with learning disabilities who exhibit concerning sexual behaviours.

Social workers seeking care placements for children have to make careful judgements in relation to how much information about a young person is passed on to other professionals. They need to balance the young person's right to privacy in relation to sexual behaviour or abuse and the placement family's or residential unit's right to be fully informed of potential care needs and risks. These decisions are often made in the context of placement scarcity and the reluctance carers may have to accommodate children and young people with a history of sexual behaviour or abuse. The anxiety which is provoked in adults by children's sexuality is often managed through silence and denial. Social workers, practising within a legal framework, need to be able to contemplate and discuss young people's sexual thoughts, feelings and behaviours, while teams and managers need to provide an environment where these taboo-laden subjects may be aired in order that appropriate assessments and decisions are made.

Sexuality and Older People

Despite a significant increase in the older population, there is still a reluctance to consider older people as sexual beings, with specific sexual and intimacy needs.

Older people who come into residential care may have partners who are still living in the couple's home. In this situation both people are facing significant losses which need to be taken on board as one person is admitted to residential care. The loss of separation, physical ability, independence, company, social networks and privacy are all present and will have implications for the way in which both people in the couple manage the transition. Residential care and nursing homes have few facilities for couples, whether the relationship is part of a person's life already or has developed within the care home. Admission to residential care also poses challenges for privacy in relation to personal care, the meeting of intimate sexual needs and control of private space. The personal and professional attitudes of care staff in relation to older people as sexual beings who are of a different generation with its own social mores further complicates this dynamic.

Working with people with dementia poses challenges as some people may begin to display sexually uninhibited behaviour towards staff and other residents. Not only does this cause distress in the living environment but family members and friends will need support in witnessing these unexpected and often shocking interactions.

Sexual Abuse and Residential Care

There are three reasons for service users to expect the highest of standards in these contexts of care. First, when children or vulnerable adults are entrusted to care provided or purchased for their safety, they have an undeniable right to an assurance that they will be as safe as humanly possible. Secondly, care systems should alleviate the adversity already experienced by service users, not compound it. Thirdly, service users in residential settings are particularly vulnerable, as an abuser operating in this context is likely to gain access to large numbers of children or vulnerable adults to abuse, and some abusers may deliberately gravitate to social care work for this reason. Police checks will identify only a small number of abusers since, in common with sexual abuse in other contexts, the abuse is more likely to go unreported and the abuser undetected.

Social Work with Sex Offenders

Social work with alleged and convicted sex offenders is a particularly challenging area of practice in which practitioners need to be highly aware of their motivations and the potential impact of the work on themselves. The persistent topicality of sex offender-focused stories in the media, epitomized by 'naming and shaming' campaigns, highlights the extent to which the sex offender has become the predominant 'other' in the public mind. People quickly take up polarized positions in relation to the risks offenders may pose: for some, offenders should be given the benefit of the doubt, regarded as humans who had lapsed and should be forgiven, or are even seen as the victims of malicious false accusers; for others, all offenders pose ongoing extreme risks such that their rights and freedoms should be significantly curtailed. Social workers are required to work on a daily basis with the risks inherent in the assessment, care and rehabilitation of sex offenders. They have to relate in a meaningful and helpful way to a person who is entitled to respect and consideration, yet who has also committed (or allegedly committed) deeply disturbing acts against vulnerable others and may continue to be dangerous in this respect. Managing the anxieties associated with the risks, uncertainties and dual responsibilities in this situation, without resort to stereotyping, punitive thinking or emotional dissociation, is no mean feat.

Sexuality in Social Work Training and Organizations

Within the social work training context, the learning environment needs to address both process and content – not only what is taught about sexuality but how it is taught. The creation of a safe, boundaried yet challenging learning environment is crucial, so that both tutors and students can develop their self-awareness on this topic of significance for personal identity and professional practice. Decisions that tutors and students make about how open they are about their sexual orientation, for example, raise important questions. The assumption of heterosexuality is pervasive. To be out at work as a gay, lesbian or bisexual tutor or student is both a personal decision and a political act. Some would argue that not to come out is colluding with the oppression which is being challenged through anti-oppressive practice and is itself a form of internalized homophobia. A counterargument is that uncertainty caused by not revealing sexual preference might be more effective in challenging expectations and assumptions.

Since December 2003 an individual is now protected from discrimination on the grounds of their sexual orientation under the Employment Equality (Sexual Orientation) Regulations 2003. Previous equality acts did not address this type of discrimination specifically. In recent years, as it has become more acceptable for LGBT social workers to be open about their sexual orientation in the workplace, an unspoken assumption has emerged in some teams that LGBT staff are more confident in dealing with sexual issues because of their personal development in coming to terms with their own sexuality. An unequal division of labour may occur where the service users for whom sexuality issues are more prominent are allocated to the lesbian and gay social workers who are seen to be, and may see themselves as, more comfortable dealing with sexual issues. The potential for ghettoization, discrimination and reinforcement of stereotypes is evident.

A healthy social work team in a practice setting or in the academic context is one where gender and sexuality issues can be addressed, not only in relation to the service users, but also in relation to the dynamics of the team itself, providing opportunities to address the unspoken assumptions and possible taboos which may underlie the team's day-to-day operation.

Conclusion

Although not explicit in the new professional standards and codes of practice, social workers have a personal and professional responsibility to work on their own issues around sex, sexual relationships and sexuality if they are to practise in a responsible and ethical way. This demands a high level of self-awareness, being comfortable with the language of sexual expression and being able to talk explicitly about sex. This will inevitably mean that long-held views may be challenged but, equally importantly, it means that the social worker will be more open to others who are struggling to express doubt, distress and anxiety in relation to sexual matters. None of this is easy. It is likely to be fraught and messy at times. It will, however, go a long way towards ensuring that social work clients and social workers themselves are understood and supported in matters relating to their sexuality and sexual relationships.

Five Key Points

- Training on issues relating to sex, sexuality and sexual relationships is crucial for ethical social work practice.
- A high level of self-awareness in relation to sexuality is important for ethical social work practice.
- Social workers need to consider sexuality issues in different contexts and across the life course.
- Sexuality offers an important arena for discussion and exploration of issues of difference, diversity and power.
- Sexually abusive behaviour occurs in a myriad of ways in social work organizations.

Three Questions

? What personal work are you aware you need to do in the area of sex, sexuality and sexual relationships in order to enable you to practise more effectively?
? How might social work practice around sexuality and sexual relationships take into account issues relating to difference, power and diversity?
? What professional boundaries in relation to sexuality have you encountered in your practice? How have these been addressed by you by the organization in which your work took place?

Further reading

1   Richardson, D. (2000) *Rethinking Sexuality*. London: Sage.
2   Wilton, T. (2000) *Sexualities in Social Care: A Textbook*. Buckingham: Open University Press.
3   Dominelli, L. (2002b) *Anti-Oppressive Social Work Theory and Practice*. London: Palgrave Macmillan.

CHAPTER 4.7

Psychology and Social Work

Brigid Daniel

Psychology is often defined as 'the scientific study of behaviour'. It is essentially a discipline or field of study that uses scientific methods to develop a body of knowledge about human behaviour. This knowledge is then applied by clinical, educational and occupational psychologists.

The spread of subdisciplines and theoretical strands can be bewildering but what does characterize psychology, is the emphasis upon an empirical approach that involves systematic, scientific and objective observations. Such observations may be obtained in many different ways that can be broadly classified into three types:

- Non-experimental methods that obtain correlational data to help find patterns of behaviour and include, for example, interviews, surveys and case studies.
- Experimental methods that look for causes of behaviour by varying one or more independent variable.
- Quasi-experimental methods that also explore causation by measuring variables that cannot be directly manipulated, for example by comparing younger and older people's memory skills.

Whatever the method, psychology aims to be rigorous. In this respect it has much to offer the current social work endeavour to move towards evidence-based practice.

Social workers are people who work with people. At the very heart of their work lies the ability to use interpersonal skills, based upon their knowledge of human functioning, to help, support, protect and empower people in distress. Therefore, psychology is fundamental, both as a tool for practice and for understanding the dynamics of practice. Consider the following:

A social worker visits a household after an anonymous referral alleging that the mother of the children is a drug addict and that the children are neglected. At the house three generations of the family are encountered: two children who appear undernourished, to have very limited language skills and to be out of parental control; the father, who is known to have a criminal record for violent behaviour, who looks deeply unhappy and says nothing; the mother who speaks to the social worker, but whose speech is very slurred; the father's mother who is very unkempt and appears confused.

From the first contact a number of questions might go through the social worker's mind:

- Are the children developmentally delayed?
- Has the mother a problem with drugs?
- Is the father depressed?
- Is the father's mother showing signs of senile dementia?
- What is the motivation of the anonymous caller?

Psychology can offer information about each of these issues. The broad academic subdivisions that offer most to social work include developmental psychology, social psychology and abnormal psychology. Most social workers will be uncomfortable with the term 'abnormal' psychology and may prefer to use the operational term 'clinical' psychology.

A different set of questions relate to the areas that would be most useful for the social worker to explore when making the assessment and deciding how to intervene:

- Is the mother physiologically addicted to drugs?
- Are there ways in which the parental environment maintains the children's difficult behaviour?
- Is the father's depression related to negative thoughts and beliefs?
- Could the mother's own childhood have affected her current behaviour?
- Would it be helpful to allow the grandmother space to describe her views about her situation?

Psychology has developed five main theoretical approaches to the study of behaviour: biological, behaviourist, cognitive, psychodynamic and humanist. All five of these theoretical approaches have influenced social work and all are associated with particular methods of intervention. The subdisciplines already described have all, to a greater or lesser degree, been approached from each of these five theoretical directions. It is this complex interweaving of broad areas of study and different approaches to study that can make psychology a rather bewildering discipline from which to garner clear messages for practice. The situation is further complicated by the fact that a different theoretical approach can be used to guide intervention than was used to understand the reason for the problem.

A final set of questions is:

- What impact will the social worker's first impressions have upon future decisions and actions?
- Do the parents have any particular stereotype of, or prejudice against, social workers?

- How will the social worker and other professionals interact at any subsequent meetings?

Social psychology can help provide insight into these questions that relate to the underlying factors impinging upon the process of social work.

In summary, therefore, psychology underpins social work in three main ways:

1 It provides a wealth of information about human functioning, including development across the lifespan, social interactions and psychopathology.
2 It offers a number of theoretical strands that can be used both to guide assessment and to plan intervention.
3 It illuminates the kind of common psychological errors that can impinge upon, and undermine, effective practice.

The Biological Approach

The biological approach is based upon materialism, that is, the view that the mind and body cannot be split. The assumption is that all behaviour has a physiological basis and that the key to understanding human behaviour lies in studying human biology. Physiological psychologists study all aspects of human biology, but the primary focus has been upon the study of the central nervous system and related systems.

Different areas of the brain that relate to particular functions have been mapped. The effects of head injuries that damage specific areas of the brain provide further evidence of the links between brain activity and behaviour. The effects of different drugs on mood and behaviour help with the understanding of chemical processes in the brain. It may seem that such information is relevant only to the medical profession, but for example, it can help the social worker in the above scenario to know that the grandparent's confusion may have a physiological basis so that appropriate referral for further assessment can be made. Similarly, an understanding of the physiological effects of addiction to and withdrawal from drugs can guide the provision of appropriate support.

The effects of the mind on the body can be illustrated by the work on the physiological impact of stressful life events. There is a significant link between the number of life events a person experiences and the likelihood of developing some form of physical illness. The current view is that a range of social and environmental factors impact upon the body's immune functions in a way that increases vulnerability to illness.

People with a history of childhood abuse have a higher risk of developing post-traumatic stress disorder in response to trauma in adulthood, perhaps due to the physiological effects of childhood trauma. Social workers are not in a position to diagnose or treat physiological effects but the knowledge that these processes occur can help the planning of prompt intervention to reduce trauma in childhood and in the recognition of the potential need for support for adult survivors of childhood trauma. The social worker in the case scenario can be helped by the knowledge that severe childhood neglect can lead to developmental abnormalities in the neuronal pathways in the brain.

Much clinical psychology is underpinned by advances in drug treatments for mental disorders such as depression and schizophrenia. The efficacy of such drug treatments attests to the biological underpinnings of some mental disorders although the details of the physiological aspects are not fully understood.

The 'nature–nurture' debate about the relative impact of inherited characteristics and of environmental influences has a long history. A range of methods have been used to study genetic influences including twin studies that allow comparisons of variations in characteristics between identical and non-identical twins; and the comparison of characteristics between twins reared together and reared apart.

This area of study has been associated with vigorous and, at times, acrimonious debate because of the ways that genetic arguments have been (and, in some cases, continue to be) used to justify classist, sexist and racist views. There is now a general consensus amongst psychologists with the interactionist view that both genetic and environmental factors affect behaviour.

The notion that behaviour such as criminal behaviour has a genetic component is a highly influential one. Eysenck (1977), for example, believed that much of personality is due to variations along two innate personality dimensions, neuroticism and extraversion, and that people who score highly on both are most likely to become involved in criminal activity because they are impulsive and do not respond well to reward and punishment. The belief that criminal behaviour has a strong genetic component leads to the view that the best response is containment but it is a theoretical approach that is not drawn upon heavily within criminal justice social work.

Behaviourist Approach

The behaviourist approach is based upon the assumption that behaviour is learnt and shaped as a result of environmental circumstances. This approach attempts to explain behaviour by studying observable responses rather than by looking for internal processes. Those practitioners who work from behaviourist beliefs apply the principles of learning when trying to change behaviour patterns. Two main strands of empirical work have contributed to the current state of knowledge about learning. One springs from Pavlov's work on classical conditioning and the other from Skinner's work on operant conditioning.

Pavlov's ground-breaking work began in the early 1900s. He was initially studying digestive processes in dogs and showed that salivation was a reflex response to the arrival of food. He then tried ringing a bell every time the food was presented. In subsequent tests the dog would salivate at the sound of the bell, without the presence of food. In behavioural terms, the dog normally shows an unconditioned response (salivation) to an unconditioned stimulus (food), in the presence of a neutral stimulus. Subsequently, after the process of classical conditioning the dog shows a conditioned response (salivation) to the conditioned stimulus (bell ringing). From this very simple paradigm have sprung a myriad of variations and an explanation for the development of phobias. Wolpe (1973) developed a treatment for phobias that is still widely used. Based on the fact that two reflexes cannot co-exist, systematic desensitization aims to replace the fear reflex (conditioned response) to the feared object with a relaxation reflex.

Operant conditioning describes the way in which voluntary behaviour (as opposed to reflex behaviour) changes as a result of environmental consequences. On the basis of his experiments on cats Skinner (1958) proposed that the probability of a voluntary response increasing depends upon it being reinforced by some type of reinforcer. This is now known as the ABC approach, in which Antecedents cue the start of Behaviour that has a Consequence that reinforces it. Skinner believed that all behaviour could be understood by looking in detail at the contingency of reinforcement, that is, the way in which behaviour depends on the reinforcer. The system of reinforcers is quite complex and is frequently misunderstood or simplified. The simplest types are a reward to increase behaviour (positive reinforcer) or a punishment to decrease behaviour (negative reinforcer).

Operant conditioning techniques have been applied in many ways in social work. Behaviour that appears bizarre can often be understood when a careful analysis of the consequences is carried out. For example, the children in the scenario may be receiving positive reinforcement for demanding behaviour in the form of additional attention from the parents. The most effective intervention is not to remove attention, but to increase the amount of attention during times when behaviour is more desirable.

Cognitive Approach

The cognitive approach seeks to describe the processes that mediate between external stimuli and behaviour. It grew from a sense that behaviourism could not fully explain phenomena such as insight. It is a disparate theoretical approach that includes the study of memory, perception, language, problem-solving, social cognitions and so on.

The study of memory has distinguished between the processes of recognition of previously seen information and recall of previously stored information. Memory is currently understood to consist of three stages, sensory memory, that is an initial buffer; short-term memory, which only has a short retention span; and long-term memory. Such concepts are used in clinical psychology to help identify the type of memory loss in brain damage or dementia. Such knowledge will also be helpful for the social worker planning care for a client with memory problems.

Memory recall occurs by a combination of retrieval and reconstruction. The study of such processes and the ways that context and suggestion can affect them are useful for social workers. For example, there is a considerable body of work on the reliability of child witness testimony that is crucial for child abuse cases. Such evidence suggests that in some circumstances children's memories may be better than adults' for information that is very familiar or distinctive to them. Younger children tend to provide less detail and less information about events, but as they get older their accounts become similar to adult levels of free-recall. Children rarely report something that has not happened but younger, especially pre-school children, can be more susceptible to suggestion.

It is suggested by cognitive theorists that language development is based on an innate language acquisition device (Chomsky, 1972). The study of language development shows children actively working out the rules of grammar. Clinical and educational psychologists are skilled in assessing language skills; however, it would be helpful for the social worker in the scenario to have an overview of the stages of language development.

One of the most well-known cognitive theories in developmental psychology is Piaget's stage theory of cognitive development. He proposed that two processes drive development with the aim of achieving equilibrium between the world and mental representations. These are assimilation, by which new information is integrated, and accommodation, where existing representations are changed to incorporate new information. Piaget (1952) described four stages of cognitive development that culminate in the ability to think abstractly. Despite challenges to details of the theory, it remains conceptually helpful.

Kohlberg (1969) also used the cognitive approach to help with the understanding of moral reasoning. His six-stage theory proposes that children move from morality based upon obedience to those in authority towards reasoning based upon the recognition of the role of intention and of laws. Some people move towards reasoning based upon values that transcend laws. There is evidence that some young people who become involved in delinquency and aggression show immature types of moral reasoning.

Social psychology has also benefited from the cognitive approach. With a series of experiments on aggression Bandura (1973) set out to explain the role of modelling in learning. He hypothesized that imitation influenced behaviour and tested this by creating situations whereby children observed an adult acting either aggressively or non-aggressively towards a large doll. When the children were subsequently frustrated by removal of some toys, those who had observed the aggressive behaviour were more likely to behave aggressively themselves. He therefore suggested that learning can be influenced by modelling. People are more likely to imitate people they like, respect and see as successful.

Modelling is seen as one of the key factors in the development of prosocial behaviour; children whose parents act kindly are more likely to be kind themselves. Social workers can make extensive use of the theory, both to understand how some behaviour has developed and for intervention. They can, at times, themselves act as models for appropriate behaviour (Howe, 1987).

The cognitive approach to the understanding of behaviour has led to cognitive behavioural theory, one that is becoming very significant for psychologists and social workers. Researchers such as Ellis (1962) hold that behaviour is influenced by the way people perceive and think about themselves and the world. He uses an ABC approach, where the Activating event triggers a faulty Belief, that in turn triggers an emotional Consequence and problems arise from faulty cognitions. He developed rational-emotive therapy in which faulty cognitions are replaced with rational ones. Intervention based upon these principles is used in clinical psychology, especially for the treatment of depression, and increasingly in social work. The approach is also helpful for understanding low self-esteem and self-efficacy in children who have been abused or neglected. If children are convinced by perpetrators that they are to blame for the abuse they are likely to develop faulty cognitions about being bad and guilty. Intervention can focus on changing these cognitions.

Psychodynamic Approach

To many, psychology is equated with the psychodynamic approach, so powerful has its influence been (Freud, 1910). It was also the first psychological theory that social workers drew upon. Fundamental to Freud's approach was the attempt to explain the internal processes that motivate behaviour. Freud's belief was one of psychic determinism, that is, that all behaviour has a cause that is to be found in the mind. As a result of his work with patients with hysteria he postulated that the mind has a conscious aspect which contains all the thoughts and feelings that we are aware of; and a subconscious part that has two levels: the preconscious from which thoughts and feelings can be accessed by choice, and the unconscious that holds repressed thoughts and feelings. According to Freud, the personality consists of three parts. The id, largely in the subconscious, is the source of the basic drives of libido and aggression and is governed by the pleasure principle. The superego, most of which is conscious, holds the internalized views of authority figures and acts as the 'conscience' trying to inhibit the id's drives. The ego, largely conscious, mediates between the id, the superego and the outer world. In order to cope with the tensions resulting from competing demands of the id, superego and outer world, the ego deploys a range of defence mechanisms. Anna Freud developed the notion of defence mechanisms further (1958).

Freud located adult pathology within faulty psychosexual development. He delineated five stages in the development of the expression of sexual drive energy: the oral, anal, phallic, latency and genital. At each stage the child has to resolve conflicts between the id, ego, superego and outer world. The way that the parent responds to the child is crucial to the successful resolution of conflicts. Problems of development are the result of the maladaptive use of defence mechanisms.

The psychodynamic approach has influenced all disciplines of psychology. Developmental psychologists have used Freud's theories to explore the impact of early experiences upon the development of adult personality. The theory that aggression is an innate drive has been employed by social psychologists attempting to understand conflict. Clinical psychology has drawn upon the view that dysfunction is due to unhealthy defence mechanisms.

Two main other strands of psychodynamic theorizing have affected social work. One strand, known as ego psychology, is represented by Erikson. He incorporated cultural factors and devised eight psychosocial stages characterized by conflicts, beginning with the trust versus mistrust conflict in the first year. Many social workers find Erikson's (1959) stages helpful in guiding their practice. For example, the worker in the scenario might consider whether the grandparent has problems with the final conflict of integrity versus despair.

The other strand, known as object relations, focused on the early development of the ego in personal relationships with significant others. Bowlby's attachment theory is from this tradition and has been hugely influential in social work theory and practice (Bowlby, 1969, 1971). Although his initial emphasis upon the primacy of the mother has since been challenged, the idea that children need a secure attachment for healthy development underpins much child care and protection work. It is highly unlikely that the social worker in the scenario would not be beginning to assess the children's relationships with the parents.

Yelloly (1980) provides a detailed account of the influence of psychoanalysis upon social work. She asserts that psychoanalytical thinking led to a more compassionate approach to mental illness and criminal behaviour because it challenged the Victorian view of people as morally autonomous that was associated with a culture of blame and censure. It also underpinned the development of case work, a technique that is still used. Yelloly (1980, pp. 121–2) lists six ways in which the social work value system was affected:

1 the primacy given to affective (rather than cognitive) elements of behaviour;
2 the central role ascribed to unconscious psychological determinants of behaviour;
3 the greater emphasis given to inner psychological processes than to social factors in explaining behaviour;
4 the stress on infantile life and its importance for the development of a personality;
5 a heightened sensitivity to psychopathology;
6 a belief in rationality, and a reliance on insight as a major strategy of intervention in therapeutic change.

Humanist Approach

In contrast to Freud's theory, the humanist approach is optimistic. It is also phenomenological in that it states that to understand behaviour it is necessary to understand the person's individual subjective experience. Behaviour is not determined purely by biology or by past experiences, rather people have a sense of purpose, are free and act intentionally. The empirical evidence to support this approach is largely gathered from case studies.

Rogers (1951) and Maslow (1954) are two of the best known humanist psychologists. Rogers identified the actualizing tendency which is the human drive for growth and self-enhancement. Each individual has cognitive structures for the 'self' and for an 'ideal self' that represents what one aspires to be. When the self and the ideal self are similar the individual experiences a state of congruence, but when they are very different the experience is of incongruence. The development of congruence is supported by social factors:

• the need for positive regard;
• conditions of worth – self or other imposed conditions for the earning of positive regard;
• introjection of values – incorporation of conditions imposed by others into the ideal self.

The best conditions for growth are:

• unconditional positive regard;
• openness (or warmth);
• empathy.

These concepts are applied in clinical practice. Rogers developed client-centred practice (later person-centred) based on the premise that the client knows what is wrong and what needs to change. The helping process hinges upon developing a relationship of equals and by aiming to provide the conditions of worth.

The concept of respect for the person and understanding of the subjective experience is a helpful model for practice, for example with people with disabilities, because it is based on a partnership rather than paternalistic model. It is also a common model for play therapy with abused and neglected children.

Maslow's focus was upon healthy rather than pathological personality development. He suggested that people's behaviour is motivated by a hierarchy of needs. First, there are those that drive behaviour by their absence. These deficiency motives are:

- physiological;
- safety;
- love and belongingness;
- esteem.

Overlaid on these are metaneeds for growth that impel the individual on a path of *self-actualization.*

Within social psychology both Roger's and Maslow's theories propose that violent behaviour is neither an innate drive, nor a simple behavioural response, but is the result of making a choice to respond aggressively. Maslow's theory has been applied to the understanding of the role of unmet needs in both victim and perpetrator psychology in criminal justice (Ainsworth, 2000).

Table 1 maps out the interactions between the different theoretical approaches and the different disciplines, with some practice examples.

Process of Social Work

Precisely because social workers are people working with people, their own psychological make-up affects the process of social work. The cognitive approach to social psychology has shown that in any human interaction people make cognitive short-cuts. Whilst helpful in allowing quicker information processing, such shortcuts undermine objectivity. They include:

- selective attention;
- group polarization;
- stereotyping.

Another is the fundamental attributional error: the tendency to underestimate the influence of situational factors when interpreting other people's behaviour and to overestimate the importance of internal factors.

In a study of the reports of enquiries into child deaths, Munro (1999) found a number of common psychological errors of evaluation that can have potentially fatal consequences:

Table 1 *Theoretical approaches and disciplines*

Approach	Causes of behaviour	Treatment	Examples		
			Developmental	*Social*	*Clinical*
Biological	Physiological	Treat physiological causes	Appreciate physiological effects of childhood trauma	Contain criminals	Refer those with mental health problems for drug treatment
Behaviourist	Environmental reinforcement	Create an environment where reinforcers support required behaviour	Use behaviour management for conduct disorder in children	Use positive reinforcement to encourage pro-social behaviour	Behaviour modification for phobias
Cognitive	Cognitive processes	Replace negative automatic thoughts with rational reasoning	Change thoughts and beliefs underlying low self-esteem in abused children	Guard against attribution errors of assessment	Help a person with depression to overcome negative thoughts
Psychodynamic	Unhealthy defence mechanisms due to problems of psychosexual development	Develop insight into causes of behaviour	Ensure that a child has the opportunity to develop at least one secure attachment	Help a violent criminal to sublimate aggressive drive through art	Help an anxious person to gain insight into the impact of childhood trauma
Humanist	Incongruence between what people feel they are and what they feel they should be; unmet needs	Provide conditions for growth; ensuring needs are met	Provide non-directive therapy for a traumatized child	Help a criminal to find appropriate ways to meet needs	Help a person with low self-esteem to become self-confident

- being resistant to changing one's mind, and failing to revise risk assessments;
- paying greater attention to evidence that supports one's own beliefs;
- looking for evidence to support one's beliefs;
- being less critical of supporting evidence than of challenging evidence.

Thus, social work can benefit from psychological insights into the ways that human functioning can impact upon professional functioning.

Pitfalls of Drawing Exclusively upon Psychology

Although it is clear that psychology has much to offer social work, the wholesale adoption of psychological theory is not without potential problems. For example, there is a tendency to individualize problems and locate them within the person, whilst not paying sufficient attention to wider factors. This tendency has been described by Rose (1985) as the 'psy complex'. So, a further set of questions that the social worker could ask about the family in the scenario is:

- Is the family's income adequate to clothe and feed two children?
- Is the accommodation suitable for their needs?
- What access do the parents have to formal and informal support services?
- Do the family members feel integrated into the community?

Because psychology is based heavily upon the construction of norms, there is a danger that people who deviate from the norm are considered to be 'abnormal', even though a norm is only an average of the spread of possibilities. When the norm becomes that which is desired and normative there is a danger of labelling people as deviant, even when they represent part of the natural diversity of human beings.

This has particularly been the case when it comes to the understanding of the psychology of black people (Robinson, 1995). The flourishing of a black perspective in psychology is one attempt to address this problem, and the challenge for social workers is to ensure that they draw upon this material and avoid perpetuating institutional racism.

Potential

Psychology does, clearly, offer a huge amount to social work, but the potential is probably not fully realized. Training in social work covers some psychology, but it is such a vast subject that only some of the basic principles of psychology and some areas such as human development can be addressed. However, it can be guaranteed that for every human problem the social worker encounters there will be a body of relevant psychological research.

Five Key Points

- Psychology is the scientific study of behaviour and is characterized by empirical research.
- Social work can make use of three main disciplines of developmental, social and cognitive psychology.
- Psychology underpins social work in three ways: by providing evidence-based knowledge, by offering theoretical approaches and by helping with the understanding of the process of practice.
- The five main theoretical approaches are biological, behaviourist, cognitive, psychodynamic and humanist.
- The use of a psychological approach must be balanced by knowledge from sociology.

Three Questions

? What arguments are there to support and refute Nicolson and Bayne's (1990) statement that 'social work is a branch of applied psychology'?

? How can social workers ensure that their use of psychological theory does not lead them to individualize problems to the exclusion of consideration of wider ecological influences?

? There is no doubt about the lessons that social work can learn from psychology, but in what ways could social work influence the direction of psychological research?

Further reading

1   Milner, J. and O'Byrne, P. (2002) *Assessment in Social Work*. Basingstoke: Palgrave Macmillan.
2   Glassman, W. E. and Hadad, M. (2004) *Approaches to Psychology*. Buckingham: Open University Press.
3   Nicolson, P., Bayne, R. and Owen, J. (2006) *Applied Psychology for Social Workers,* 3rd edn. Basingstoke: Palgrave Macmillan.

Essentials

of Social Work

Policy Practice

Cynthia J. Rocha

 John Wiley & Sons, Inc.

Published by John Wiley & Sons, Inc., Hoboken, New Jersey.
Published simultaneously in Canada.

Wiley Bicentennial Logo: Richard J. Pacifico

For general information on our other products and services please contact our Customer Care Department within the United States at (800) 762-2974, outside the United States at (317) 572-3993 or fax (317) 572-4002.

Wiley also publishes its books in a variety of electronic formats. Some content that appears in print may not be available in electronic books. For more information about Wiley products, visit our web site at www.wiley.com.

Library of Congress Cataloging-in-Publication Data

Rocha, Cynthia J.
    Essentials of social work policy practice / by Cynthia J. Rocha.
        p. cm. — (Essentials of social work practice series)
    ISBN-13: 978-0-471-75220-2 (pbk.)
    1. Social work education. 2. Social case work—Management. 3. Social services—Political aspects. 4. Social policy. I. Title.
    HV11.R52 2007
    361.3 2—dc22

                                                            2006037550

Printed in the United States of America.

10 9 8 7 6 5 4 3 2 1

One

INTRODUCTION TO COMMUNITY-BASED POLICY PRACTICE

RATIONALE AND DESCRIPTION OF POLICY PRACTICE

Although there is not complete agreement on what constitutes policy practice, there is general agreement that social workers must assume policy roles and learn to perceive policy practice as among the skills of a practicing social worker, not the purview of a policy expert. Bruce Jansson first developed the concept of policy practice for social workers in the mid-1980s as a specific intervention designed to make changes in the political arena (Jansson, 2003). Wyers (1991) and Figueira-McDonough (1993) began calling for an increased recognition of policy practice interventions as a necessary continuum of skills for social workers to help clients at larger systems levels. There is now a clearer understanding that social workers may be called on to utilize policy practice skills, regardless of their specialized areas of interest. For the purpose of this book, policy practice is defined as a change approach that uses advocacy and community practice techniques to change programs and policies at multiple systems levels, targeting communities, local, state, and federal governments, agencies, bureaucracies, and the courts.

Conceptualizing Policy Practice

There are many ways that authors have conceptualized the various components of policy practice; as political social work, class advocacy, political advocacy, community practice, social action, and legislative advocacy, to name a few. In 1991, Wyers attempted to integrate some of the micro- and macro-approaches to policy practice by defining a model that included a continuum of policy practice skills, including (a) a policy expert—one who conducts policy analysis and provides expert knowledge and skills pertaining to the policy arena, (b) the social worker as a change agent working in an external environment, meaning that she or he works outside of her or his organization advocating for legislative initiatives, working in policy development, or working for change in services, (c) working for change in his or her own agency, or (d) being a policy conduit for change, meaning being an expert in an area and providing education on needed changes to policymakers. Wyers concluded by stating that "all social workers need to participate in the modification of social policy that is harmful to clients and the elimination of policy deficits by working for new policy" (Wyers, 1991, p. 246). McInnis-Dittrich (1994) agreed that the meaning of professional social work, by definition, means integrating social welfare policy and social work practice.

However, most definitions of policy practice are largely defined by interventions designed to change policies in legislative, agency, or community settings from a largely macro practice perspective. Figueira-McDonough (1993) defines policy practice as the formal process of influencing both legislative and judicial decision making, as well as constituency-based patterns of influence in communities and organizations. She outlines four methods of policy practice in these arenas: legislative advocacy, reform through litigation, social action, and policy analysis. Jansson (2003) defines policy practice as efforts to change policies in legislative, agency, and community settings. He further differentiates policy advocacy from policy practice by stating that policy advocacy focuses on performing policy practice methods with powerless groups, to improve their resources and opportunities. However, he admits that he uses the terms interchangeably throughout much of his discussion.

A related term, which has been used repeatedly in the literature is, *political social work*. Political social work has been defined differently depending on the author. In a discussion of these differing definitions, Fisher (1995) suggested that "policy implementation, electoral activity, community organizing—macro methods—were what most people in the profession understood as political social work" (p. 198). This approach to political social work focuses largely on a more traditional sense of politics, such as "legislation, the executive branch, interest groups, lobbying, working with the media, and running for office" (Hoefer, 1999, p. 75). Contrary to this approach is a more integrated approach that sees all social work as political social work, regardless of what level of practice, micro or macro, one focuses her or his interventions. For this integrated approach, political social work is seen as social work based on a politicized understanding of social welfare, and methods of practice are integrated. Thus, the goal is to train politicized social workers who see issues of power and justice as central to understanding and addressing social problems, as well as confronting client needs.

Many authors have used the term *advocacy* in their definition of what I consider policy practice skills. Let me first emphasize that advocacy related to policy practice must be distinguished from case advocacy because of the systemic nature of the change. For example, if a social worker has a client who experiences a problem maneuvering through the maze of social programs and we assist her or him in gaining resources, then we are performing case advocacy. But if we see client after client having the same problem, then it becomes a waste of valuable time and resources to individually advocate for each client. That is when policy practice comes into play. We want to advocate making a policy change so that all of the clients can receive these services, and we do not have the time to advocate for each one of them individually. It is time to perform policy practice.

But even within the description of class advocacy, there is a rather complex array of definitions of various attributes of advocacy. For example, Schneider and Lester (2001) differentiate in great detail their definition of advocacy as the "mutual representation of a client or clients or a cause in a forum, attempting to systematically influence decision making in an unjust or unresponsive system[s]" (p. 65) from other forms of social work practice. For example, they suggest that advocacy is a form of social action, incorporating many of the concepts of system level change and influence, but it is specifically responsible to a client or client system in a forum within an exclusive and mutual relationship. Distinguishing their definition from community organizing (CO), they state that CO is primarily an organizing and capacity-building function with emphasis on collective support through education and participation to address common concerns.

Ezell (2001) created a typology of different forms of advocacy, indicating that there was actually little variation in their meaning, although scholars have seemed to have a preference for one or the other on a theoretical level. He includes class advocacy, an intervention on behalf of a group of clients who share the same problem; systems advocacy, changing policies and practices affecting all persons in a certain group; policy advocacy, efforts to influence those who work with laws, public programs, or court decisions; political advocacy, which appears the same as class, policy, and systems advocacy; legislative advocacy, promoting and influencing legislation; and community advocacy, organizing and educating on behalf of communities who have similar problems or needs but may not be known to each other.

It is academically important to build theories and methods around various policy practice and advocacy definitions. Rapid Reference 1.1 summarizes the various concepts of what we have included under the larger

≡ Rapid Reference 1.1

Concepts Used to Describe Policy-Related Social Work

Policy practice	Legislative advocacy
Policy advocacy	Reform through litigation
Political advocacy	Policy analysis
Political social work	Social action
Class advocacy	Community organizing
System advocacy	Community development

rubric of political social work. Much of this work targets advocacy at the legislative, judicial, community, and agency settings. It also largely differentiates itself from community techniques of community organizing, community development, and social action (with the exception of Figueira-McDonough). For the purposes of skill building, it is important to use whatever techniques work for a given problem with a given population. And while I think the theory building that has occurred at the academic level of policy practice and advocacy is important, I am more interested in pursuing the next level of how to reach the goals to change a system that needs to be changed, and learning to use whatever skills are necessary and appropriate to make those changes occur. The goal of this book, therefore, is to move away from theoretical and conceptual discussions of policy practice and focus on the skill sets necessary to put it into practice. In some instances, methods and skills of community work are necessarily integrated into more traditional views of policy practice, because mobilizing the community is part of how to reach people, and people are needed in order to work in policy practice at a grassroots level.

WHY COMMUNITY-BASED POLICY PRACTICE?

In this book, policy practice encompasses all of the work that social workers do to try to change systems for the betterment of their clients, neighborhoods, and communities. The focus in this book, however, is on the specific skills needed to change policy from a community-based, grassroots perspective. While most policy practice is discussed in the realm of the larger political system, there is a need to look at policy practice from the ground up. Policy at all levels affects people, their neighborhoods, and their local communities. Regardless of where the policy originates, be it local government, a school system, an agency, the county, the state, or in the courts, it ultimately affects individual people. Oftentimes we believe that policy is too large, too complex, and too removed from the people for us to be able to have an influence. But the fact is that most policy that affects our day-to-day lives is very much within the realm of our influence.

After 12 years of working with various task groups on specific local, state, and federal policies, it has become abundantly clear that with the proper planning and skills, a small group of motivated people can make major changes that can positively impact entire communities. There are generic skills that can be used to target any system of change, including mobilizing the community around an issue, using the media to inform both the public and decision makers of problems or policy solutions, and using technology to get the word out to as many people as possible about issues that need to be addressed. Other skills are more particular to a certain target system, such as testifying before local and state committees or participating in grassroots campaign movements. The point is that individuals and members of local communities are very powerful in influencing the decisions that affect our daily lives, regardless of the level of government or bureaucracy from which they stem. But we need a skill set, a way to plan the changes to make them effective, and an understanding of who to target to make the change, and that is the primary focus of this book.

POLICY PRACTICE IN THE COMMUNITY AS A RESPONSE TO DEVOLUTION

This book emphasizes the community as a good beginning point to do many different types of policy practice. It is important to understand how the political climate has changed over the last 20 years that makes it more important to target local levels of government and to use grassroots approaches to target higher and more distant public officials. Linhorst (2002) recounts the history of federalism, which has given way to the decentralization of decision making to the local and state levels of government. Federalism is a system of government that divides responsibilities of governing among various levels of government. In the United States, responsibilities have traditionally been divided horizontally across the executive, legislative, and judicial branches, but also vertically among the federal, state, and local levels of government. In his historical account of federalism in this country, Linhorst explains that prior to the Great

Depression U.S. federalism was characterized by dual federalism, where clear roles were assigned to the federal and state governments, with states holding considerable power. Cooperative federalism developed after the Depression, however, because state governments needed assistance in response to adverse economic conditions. Federal power and control over programs increased drastically during this time.

Throughout the 1960s cooperative dualism existed in this country, until the current state of federalism was initiated by President Nixon. Believing that the federal government had grown too large, he provided block grants and general revenue-sharing dollars to local governments, increased uniformity in the food stamp program across states, and initiated supplemental security income. This state of federalism was dubbed "New" federalism. It did not decrease revenues to the state, but gave them more flexibility to create programs that were locally appropriate. But President Reagan took the concept of new federalism to another level, by supporting less government at all levels, devolving federal power to the states, and at the same time cutting federal social programs and reducing funds originally targeted to state and local governments. The 104th Congress (mid-1990s) took devolution even further by seeking to eliminate federal entitlement programs, reducing overall federal spending even further, and cutting taxes at the same time. Although most of the responsibility for implementing social programs has now shifted to the states, the federal government continues to be the primary funder. Much of the decision-making authority now rests with state and local governments, making it easier for agencies to create their own rules and regulations based on local mandates. Thus, the decision-making authority is much closer to home.

The social work literature is replete with research on how the way devolution has been handled has hurt the poor, decreased protection of oppressed populations, and increased the inequities in social protection between the states. However, devolution also had the consequence of bringing much of the power base and decision making back to state and local governments. Whereas in the past, policy practitioners spent much of their time working at the federal level of government, the changing nature of federalism requires social workers to adapt their policy practice to the state and local levels. One of the consequences of the new federalism is that although few initiatives have been enacted by the federal government that have helped our constituents, considerable gains have been made at the state level. Unfortunately, the research does not indicate that the new federalism has helped promote social equity or justice at the local levels, yet federal oversight is still needed to ensure that local communities meet the needs of their citizens.

With the state of new federalism, it is unlikely that the federal government is willing to provide much oversight for citizen protection. However, because many problems are community based, meaning that the problems—and often the solutions—can be found in our own communities, social workers are in a unique position to hold local communities responsible as well. As Linhorst (2002) points out, "the current phase of new federalism has devolved increased responsibility to the states, and social workers, as we have done historically, need to adapt our approach to promoting social justice" (p. 205). What social workers need is the knowledge and skills to be able to identify problems, seek out alternative solutions, and make changes that can assist as many community members as possible. Although interventions at the federal level are still important, it is an opportune time to turn our attention to state and local policies because they now have much of the decision-making authority. They are closer to home, are easier to communicate with, have a better understanding of the local problems that we encounter, and have an increased likelihood of successful policy interventions at a more local level.

POLICY PRACTICE AND THE ETHICS OF THE PROFESSION

The code of ethics is quite clear on our responsibility as a profession to perform policy practice activities. The ethical responsibility of social workers to engage in social and political change efforts is clearly set out in section 6.04a of the National Association of Social Workers' Code of Ethics (1999):

> Social workers should engage in social and political action that seeks to ensure that all people have equal access to the resources, employment, services, and opportunities they require to meet their basic human needs and to develop fully. Social workers should be aware of the impact of the political arena on practice and should advocate for changes in policy and legislation to improve social conditions in order to meet basic human needs and promote social justice.

There are six principles in the code of ethics from which the standards derive. Rapid Reference 1.2 delineates the six principles in the code. Once we realize the importance of advocating on the part of our clients, neighbors, and communities, it becomes clear that each of these six principles has something to do with policy practice. For example, principle 1 states that the primary goal is to help people in need and to address social problems. But how can we really address social problems if we do not practice

≡ Rapid Reference 1.2

Ethical Principles in the Code of Ethics of the National Association of Social Workers (1999)

1. Social workers' primary goal is to help people in need and to address social problems.
2. Social workers challenge social injustice.
3. Social workers respect the inherent dignity and worth of the person.
4. Social workers recognize the central importance of human relationships.
5. Social workers behave in a trustworthy manner.
6. Social workers practice within their areas of competence and develop and enhance their professional expertise.

policy? A personal problem becomes a social problem when it affects a large number of people. If a problem is affecting a large number of people, then something is amiss. Either a community is having economic problems of some sort that are affecting a large number of people, a policy that is supposed to support families is not working properly, or an agency that is supposed to supply a certain service is not functioning effectively. All of these issues point to a target system that needs an intervention of some sort. This is policy practice.

The goal of social justice as part of both the social work code of ethics and our profession's person-in-environment perspective has been a challenge for social workers. Although social work as a profession has made a commitment to social justice for the families we work with, social workers are often challenged because they lack skills in the strategies and techniques of policy practice needed to realize policy change. As Gordon (1994) points out, by not taking a leadership role in the formulation and implementation of the policies that affect our clients, the profession's person-in-environment perspective is largely missing from programs and services. Learning policy practice methods and skills is seen as a "necessary means to the implementation of the neglected goal of social justice" (Figueira-McDonough, 1993, p. 180). The integration of policy practice methods emphasizing social and organizational change with direct practice content is a challenge. But this integration is essential to broaden the influence that social service workers have to promote positive impacts in our clients' lives.

DOES POLICY PRACTICE REALLY WORK?

Many people, and social workers are no exception, feel helpless to try to make changes in the systems we work with, whether it is in our own agency or in a legislative body. But this book provides evidence that, with good planning and the right skill sets, changes can and do occur. The methods outlined in this book have been utilized since 1992 with social work students, and the results have been impressive (Rocha & Johnson, 1997).

Throughout this book, examples of projects that have both prevailed and failed are given, with tips on why they did or did not work.

This book is an outgrowth of not only years of teaching, but also evaluating whether the planning model works. In 2000, graduates who had taken the course and had formed task groups and used the skills in this book to try to make changes in their communities were surveyed 6 months after graduation. These graduates were compared with graduates who had taken other advanced policy practice courses, but did not have the experience of going into the community and using the planned change method (Rocha, 2000). The study assessed three dimensions of policy-related activities: (a) whether policy practice activities were valued as important tasks, (b) whether graduates felt competent in doing policy practice activities, and (c) how active the graduates were in actually performing policy practice activities since they graduated. All graduates reported valuing policy practice equally. Those with policy practice experience were significantly more likely to feel competent using the media to communicate ideas to the public, plan and implement a planned change effort, use the Internet to find policy-related information, and create computer-generated information (e.g., brochures, newsletters). Students who had policy practice experience were also significantly more likely to have worked on a specific change effort since graduation, become a member of a committee or coalition, and were more likely to organize policy activities. Thus, whether a student or practitioner, I urge the reader to put the ideas in this book to use. Activities at the end of each chapter provide added opportunities for practice.

This book provides a policy practice planning process that is familiar to both community social workers and clinicians alike because it uses similar steps as the problem-solving models that are often used with individual clients. It provides step-by-step instructions on how to put a plan into action. Each chapter describes detailed skills that can be used to bring awareness to problems, utilize resources to deal with problems, and put into action a plan to solve the problems. Many skills can be used at several levels, from local community issues, such as transportation and child care, to larger issues, such as changing laws to create more equitable distribution of resources. Each chapter presents new skill sets, depending on the system requiring change. There are many examples and illustrations, in the hope that the more we practice these skills, the more competent we feel to utilize them.

The next chapter outlines the planning stage in great detail. The following four chapters detail specific skill sets that can be used across targeted systems for change (e.g., utilizing the media, organizing coalitions). The last four chapters look at different potential target systems and provide in-depth information on particular strategies needed to intervene within these systems (e.g., local agencies, legislature). Thus, some skills are specific to a particular target system, but many of the skills from the previous chapters can be used across targeted systems. The important thing to remember is that each problem and each strategy should be analyzed carefully to assess what will likely lead to the best outcome for your clients.

SUMMARY

In an age of devolution of both resources and decision making down to the local level, social workers have greater opportunities to effect change, but also increased challenges, due to decreased resources. Policy practice skills are necessary to address these challenges and seize opportunities to make substantial differences in the lives of our clients. The skills and target systems discussed in the next chapters will provide easy-to-follow instructions on how to strategize changes in many different systems.

TEST YOURSELF

1. Provide one example of how the ethical principle of "respecting the inherent dignity and worth of the person" could be linked to policy practice.

2. Identify a social problem of interest to you. Trace backward the assistance that people are given. Where does the funding come from?

3. Identify a policy that an agency you are affiliated with has. Where does the policy originate? Is it formal or informal?

4. **Think about a specific client group that you work with. What are some of the problems they face? Do several clients face the same problems?**

5. **Remember the discussion on the difference between case and class advocacy. How different would it be to try to solve a problem for an entire group of clients, rather than one at a time?**

6. **Why has the goal of social justice in the profession's "person-in-environment perspective" been such a challenge for social workers?**

7. **Discuss the opportunities and challenges of devolution.**

8. **How has devolution impacted the way social workers must work in the policy practice arena?**

9. **Policy practice methods can be used at the local level as well as the federal level.** True or False?

10. **Policy practice methods should only be used in the legislative arena and are inappropriate for use in judicial decision making.** True or False?

Answers: 9. True; 10. False

Five

UTILIZING TECHNOLOGY IN POLICY PRACTICE

Technology has changed the face of policy practice in recent years. The ease with which we can now use the computer to create professional brochures, fliers, business cards, and newsletters can save money and time for groups and organizations that work on policy issues. Even more phenomenal is the pace at which the Internet is being used. Between 2000 and 2005, for example, Internet use among Americans went from 46 percent to 67 percent of the population who go online (Pew Charitable Trust, 2006). The use of cell phones is another technological advancement that is growing and advancing at a rapid pace. Just 10 years ago cell phones were big and bulky, expensive, and used by few in the United States. Now cell phones are small, inexpensive, digital, and can be used to text message, e-mail, and access the Internet.

This chapter will explore the pros and cons in the use of technology in policy practice and give some practical skills in using technology to advocate and organize people to participate in the policy process. We must be aware that not everyone has access to technology, and therefore our target population and the populations that we may want to partner with for policy change must be considered carefully before we embark on an exciting trip through cyberspace. But even if we find that some forms of technology will not be effective in our planning stage, there is always room for innovative and creative ways to use technology. It is simply very important to analyze where the use of technology is important, and where it may or may not have the desired outcome. These issues, along with tips on how to become more technologically savvy, will be explored in this chapter.

60

DESKTOP PUBLISHING

Most major word processing computer programs, such as Microsoft Word and WordPerfect, now have the ability to do desktop publishing. Newsletters, brochures, business cards, and other published materials can be made at home or in your office. Most programs have templates, or *wizards,* that tell you exactly how to create the material and what usually goes where.

Brochures and Fact Sheets

Brochures and fact sheets are fast and easy ways to get a message out to the public, agencies, public officials, and others. They are easy to make and look very professional. Brochures can be used to provide information about a variety of topics; they are made in such a way that there is optimal space provided to give information, and they can be mailed by simply folding them and stapling one end. The student groups at the University of Tennessee have used brochures for a variety of purposes. They have distributed brochures to school administrators and students to create awareness of the lack of handicapped access on campus and to elderly clients to provide information on how to use free drug programs. Small organizations give clients brochures that elaborate on the services they provide. The list goes on and on. The following Putting It Into Practice provides tips on where to put information in a brochure. Most word processing programs also provide templates for ease of creating brochures, as well as many other publishing materials, and some other suggestions on where to put certain information.

Don't try to fill the panels entirely with text. White (empty) spaces make the brochure more inviting and easier to read. Graphics can be added to the panel by going to the insert menu and selecting clip art to insert. Brochure panels are usually read in the order listed. While the sixth panel is the cover and gets looked at first, most people actually begin reading on the first panel, which is on the inside cover. Therefore, panels 4, 5, and 6 are the outside of the brochure and 1, 2, and 3 are the inside of the bro-

Putting It Into Practice

Brochure Panels

Panel 4	Panel 5	Panel 6
People who contributed to the activity.	If you plan to mail out your brochure, this panel will be where the address and stamp are placed. The word processing program will automatically put the return address sideways.	**Brochure Title** (clip art is nice here) Name of Organization
Panel 1	**Panel 2**	**Panel 3**
Who we are Features (the description of your product, service or organization)	What we do Benefits (the description of its benefits to your audience or clients)	Action Action (what you want people to do after reading the brochure)

chure. When the brochure is printed out there will be two pages, panels 4, 5, 6 on one page and panels 1, 2, 3 on the next. These should be copied back to back. Since panel 6 will be read first, use a picture or clip art, as it livens up the brochure and makes the reader more interested in reading on. If it is about a local event, don't forget to list the sponsors on panel 4.

Newsletters

The primary goal of a newsletter is to keep an organization's membership informed about issues affecting the group. The newsletter should reserve the first article as a cover article that gives a current update on a policy or problem that is being addressed by the members. There should also be an article regarding upcoming events and who to contact for more information. Membership forms or donation forms can appear at the bottom of the newsletter so that members and others can cut them out and return them.

Depending on what issue you are working on, a secondary purpose of the newsletter is to inform community members, other organizations, politicians, or the press of your activities. This strategy should be done with some thought. Who do you want to target besides your membership? Since some articles in the newsletter may be targeting specific state agencies, school boards, legislators, and to alert members of an upcoming action, this may not be the time to share your newsletter with just anyone. But at other times—when you are writing about accomplishments, for example—you would want to send a copy to pertinent officials or to the media.

Most word processing programs will have one or two newsletter formats to choose from. Choose a format that is easy to read. The following Putting It Into Practice gives an example of a newsletter that was produced with a template from a simple word processing program. High school students at a small, community-based nonprofit school designed a professional-looking newsletter. Note the liberal use of clip art and boxes to bring out particular requests or to highlight certain areas of the newsletter. Also note that changing the font for different sections can liven up the newsletter as well as draw attention to particular issues. Just as a side note, because the students had covered all of the articles they wanted to, and there was still a little bit of space on the second page, the dove on the back became a lot larger!

The following check list describes the pull-down menus to find templates in both Microsoft Word and WordPerfect:

✓ Microsoft Word 2003: Go to File/New and select Templates (for earlier versions of Word, select Wizards. Depending on the version of Microsoft Word that you are using, some of the

Laurel High School

Volume 1 Issue 1 | February 1999

Students Tackle Important Issues

By Joel Marshall

Laurel High School's Student Council was formed last year by students concerned with issues and problems facing the school. Some of the issues being dealt with so far are scheduling conflicts, student credit deficiencies, student education, and drug issues. The council met several times over the summer to work on changes in this year's scheduling of classes. The council has no formal membership, but is composed of students willing to exercise whatever necessary to take responsibility for the well being of the school. We find that the student council is a wonderful step towards making Laurel an even more tightly knit community.

LHS Climbing Team Hits the Top
(But Not Hard Enough to Leave a Bruise)

By Kelly Brown
Climbing Team Coach

The past few years the ten members of the LHS climbing team are again competing against many area high schools. Last year Laurel teams in second place citywide. This year we are contenders for the crown. The team has gained a good deal of support from its student body, staff, and parents, has been fund from its student body, staff, and parents has been tremendous. Please call the school (525-3883) if you would like a schedule.

If you would like to visit the school or a guest speaker, please call 525-3883 and ask for Claudia!

Family Night '98

By Charlotte Maxwell-Jones

On the eve of Oct. 29, 1998, the Laurel students and faculty hosted a presentation of some of their school-related projects and activities. Jodd Hook showed sculptures made from twisted wire and other "found" objects. Melba Ramsey displayed hand-sewn dolls based on her favorite manga (Japanese comic books) characters. The Conversational Spanish class sang "La Bamba", accompanied by Fletcher Stewart and Harold Heffner on guitar. The video making class presented some of their recent works. Bess Jefferson displayed his talent as a weaponsmith. With those and other displays of talent and plenty of good food, Family Night was deemed a great success by all involved.

--- (cut out)

If you would like to make a donation, please provide your name and address. Be sure to indicate what program you would prefer to support! Mailing address: LHS, 1020 Laurel Avenue, Knoxville, TN 37916

☐ Travel Club
☐ Area Program
☐ Other:
TOTAL:

☐ Book Climbing Team
☐ Computer Lab
☐ No Preference

Phone make all checks payable to Laurel High School. All donations are tax-deductible!

Your Name: _____
Your Address: _____
City: _____ Apt #: _____ State: _____ ZIP: _____

Laurel High School Newsletter

By Claudia White
Principal, LHS

Clear Tom is a support group designed to promote healthy choices for youth in the Knoxville community rather than alcohol and drug use. The program is designed to have a formal support group meetings and physical activities that interest the group. It is open to any teenager who has the intention and desire to stay clean from drugs and alcohol. Currently, our group participates in rock climbing, paleo-anthropological activities and massage therapy ☺

Travel Opportunities
Diversity Through Music

By Joel Marshall and Charlotte Maxwell-Jones

Four students from Laurel High School raised funds for a 3-week field trip to the United Kingdom. Traveling through England, Scotland and Wales, they visited historical landmarks, observed the surrounding cultures, and adapted to their companions' diverse traveling styles. The expedition was an overall success, and LHS will continue to have these programs available to industrious students. →

More Travel Opportunities

Spanish Trip
By Cynthia Rocha

The Conversational Spanish class is planning a road trip to Mexico on March 15, 1999. We will go through San Antonio and visit the Alamo and the Missions. We will then travel to Nuevo Laredo, Mexico, shop at the mercados, walk through the zocalos, and visit the museums. Although we have done some fundraising, we are still raising money. If you would like to donate for the trip, we would appreciate it. Or come by our yard sale this Saturday and Sunday, march 6 & 7 at Laurel!

Thanks!

--- (cut out)

We are trying to build a database of LHS student, faculty, and alumni addresses and phone numbers! Please fill out the form below and mail to Claudia White. We would like to have mailing, e-mail addresses and phone numbers on file for as many of us as possible. Thank you for your cooperation!

Name: _____
Address: _____ Apt. #: _____
City: _____ State: _____ ZIP: _____
Home Phone ( ) _____ E-Mail: _____

templates (brochures, for example) will be on the computer and others can be obtained by going online.

✓ WordPerfect 11: Go to File/New/Start New Project; under the "Create New" tab there is a pull-down menu with twenty or so options. Choose "Creative Projects" for brochures, certificates, newsletters, and greeting cards. Choose "Publish" for business cards.

Other Desktop Publishing Ideas

It's easy to be creative with desktop publishing. Fliers are fun to create to inform people about upcoming events, and pictures for fliers can be downloaded, either from your own jpeg files or from clip art that comes with most programs. Word processing programs are so advanced that professional fliers can be made that look as if you just paid a printing company to print them for you. Templates for business cards are also included in both Microsoft Word and WordPerfect.

Aside from these ideas, which have templates included in the program, there are a lot of creative ways to utilize simple programs. For example, the following Putting It Into Practice demonstrates an innovative approach that a student task force took to assist a rural county's sheriff's department deal with domestic violence cases. Anecdotal evidence by social workers in the area reported that the police were not responding to all domestic violence calls, and that those calls that were answered were oftentimes answered at a very slow pace. The task force decided to approach the sheriff to gather more information. What they found were officers who were poorly trained to deal with domestic violence and an overworked staff that saw the same families calling in time and again with no one willing to press charges.

Aside from several other strategies to assist the sheriff's department with training on domestic violence and connecting them with the women's shelter in a neighboring county, students made pocket cards that the police could carry to the residents and quietly slip into the victim's hand if she or he decided (as was often the case) not to press charges or have the

Putting It Into Practice

Domestic Violence Pocket Cards—A, Front of Card; B, Back of Card

Domestic Violence is a Crime

National Domestic
Violence Hotline
1-800-799-SAFE(7233)
1-800-787-3224 (TTD)

A

Safety Plan for Domestic Violence Victims

Safety during an explosive incident

- If an argument seems unavoidable, try to have it in a room or area where you have access to an exit. Try to stay away from the bathroom, kitchen, bedroom or any where else where weapons might be available.
- Practice how to get out of your home safely. Identify which doors, windows, elevator or stairwell would be best.
- Have a packed bag ready and keep it at a relative's or friend's home in order to leave quickly.
- Identify one or more neighbors you can tell about the violence and ask that they call the police if they hear a disturbance coming from your home.
- Devise a code word to use with your children, family, friends and neighbors when you need the police.
- Decide and plan for where you will go if you have to leave home (even if you don't think you will need to).
- Use your own instincts and judgement. If the situation is very dangerous, consider giving the abuser what he wants to calm him down.

You have the right to protect yourself until you are out of danger.
- Always remember:
YOU DON'T DESERVE TO BE HIT OR BE THREATENED!!!

Safety When Preparing to Leave

- Open a savings account and/or a credit card in your own name to start to establish or increase your independence. Think of other ways in which you can increase your independence.
- Leave money, an extra set of keys, copies of important documents, extra medicines and clothes with someone who would be able to let you stay with them or hold you money.
- Keep the shelter or hotline phone numbers close at hand and keep some change or a calling card on you at all times for emergency phone calls.
- Review your Safety Plan as often as possible in order to plan the safest way to leave your abuser. *REMEMBER:*
- *LEAVING YOUR ABUSER IS THE MOST DANGEROUS TIME!!!*

What is an Order of Protection?

It is a legal order to protect the victim from further abuse.

How to obtain an order of Protection

- Fill out a petition at the County Court Clerk's office for an order of protection and an ex parte order. They will schedule a court hearing approximately 10 days from petition date. An order is effective for one year.

√ *Be aware that the respondant will be served papers prior to the court date and has the option of participating in the court hearing.*

For More Information ...
24 Hour Emergency Housing & Other Services

Law Enforcement
Emergency   911

City Police (non-emergency)
Greeneville	639-7111
Johnson City	926-5134
Bristol	989-5600
Kingsport	246-9111
Erwin	743-1870
Elizabethton	542-4141

County Sheriff's Department:
Greene	639-3181
Washington	461-1414
Sullivan	323-5125
Carter	543-1850
Unicoi	743-1850

Safe Passage	926-7233
Safe Passage Beeper	461-0268
Abuse Alternatives	632-9093
Safe House	578-3668
CHIPS	742-0022
Contact	926-0144

B

perpetrator removed. Panels A and B show the small pocket-size card. Panel B show the amount of information that was put on the inside of the card, and that was just the inside cover! They were made by using the columns tab on WordPerfect, making two columns lengthwise and typing the information in the landscape format so the words were sideways on the page. Two cards could be made out of one piece of paper, folded. This gave four small pages that had information front and back. They also had facts about domestic violence, signs of domestic violence, options for victims of domestic violence, an outline of a safety plan, how to obtain an order of protection, and phone numbers for services for victims of domestic violence in nearby areas. All of this on a 2 × 4 inch card that could be slipped into a victim's hand without being seen. The sheriff's department really liked the card, because they felt at a loss to help the women who would call. Because the victims often refused to press charges, and the perpetrator was sometimes present, they did not feel comfortable talking to the officers, and did not know what to say except that they could take them to jail. The pocket cards gave them information they could carry with them in their shirt pocket.

POLICY PRACTICE ONLINE

Before beginning a discussion about using the Internet for policy practice, it is important to think again about the target audience and our strategies in the planning stage. Who are we targeting? How can we best use the Internet to target this agency, representative, or community? If we are going to do a public awareness campaign (see Chapter 7 for more details), for example, is the community connected to the Internet? If we are organizing a grassroots campaign around a policy issue from a low-income area, should we use a strategy that assumes the residents have access to the Internet? These are important questions to ask, because we cannot assume that people have computers, have Internet service, or have access to the Internet.

Having differential access to the Internet and the skills needed to use it refers to an issue known as the *digital divide*. The digital divide is broadly described as the gap between individuals and communities who have access to digital technology and those who do not. Steyaert (2002) outlined how access to technology replicates existing social stratification. If this is still the case, then strategies that attempt to organize poor communities online will not reach their target population. However, the divide in access has been closing as computers and Internet services have become cheaper. Between 2000 and 2005, for example, the Pew Charitable Trust (2006) found that households who use the computer in the United States increased from 62 percent to 70 percent and Internet use climbed from 46 percent to 67 percent during the same period. Rapid Reference 5.1 shows the breakdown by gender, race, and age during these two periods.

It is clear that access to computers and the Internet grew dramatically during the 5-year period between 2000 and 2005. However, it is also clear that there are still up to 42 percent of some populations without access to the Internet, and almost three-fourths of our oldest population lack access to the Internet. In 2006, the Pew survey was replicated, now including income and education in its report. As Rapid Reference 5.2 points out, while the digital divide has clearly become smaller by race and gender, there is a greater divide by age and socioeconomic status. Older Americans are much less likely to use the Internet than younger Americans. Only 53 percent of households with incomes less than $30,000 per year and only 40 percent with less than a high school education use the Internet. Steyaert's (2002) claim of the digital divide following the general stratification of society appears to continue to hold true by economic status. Those with less education are the most likely to make less money, and these two groups used the Internet the least.

There is also growing concern that the digital divide is not just about access. Even though a household may report they use the Internet, the type of use is important. It is not enough to ask whether one has access, but how the Internet is used and what the quality of access is. For example, Riley, Wersma, and Belmarez (2006) report that only 46 percent of students in

≡ *Rapid Reference 5.1*

Computer and Internet Use, 2000–2005 (%)

	2000	2005
Computer Use		
Men	64	71
Women	60	70
Whites	53	71
Blacks	51	66
Hispanics	58	72
18–29	78	84
30–49	74	80
50–64	54	72
65+	20	29
Internet Use		
Men	49	68
Women	44	65
Whites	48	67
Blacks	35	58
Hispanics	40	68
18–29	64	84
30–49	56	76
50–64	36	64
65+	12	27

Adapted from Pew Charitable Trust (2006).

metro Nashville could research term papers or find online information from home during the 2005–2006 school year. In fact, statewide surveys show that in Tennessee, 40 of 140 schools had access levels of less than 50 percent from home.

There should be caution used when deciding when and how to use the

≡ *Rapid Reference 5.2*

Percent Internet Use, by Selected Characteristics, 2006

	Internet Users
Age 18–29	88
Age 65 and older	32
Income less than $30,000 per year	53
Income $75,000 plus	91
Less than high school education	40
College education	91

Adapted from Pew Charitable Trust (2006).

CAUTION

Know your target audience and your stakeholders and discuss the pros and cons of reaching them via the Internet. The digital divide still exists and should be analyzed before attempting to use advanced technology to reach an audience that does not use it.

Internet in policy practice, particularly in terms of lower-income and elderly families. On the other hand, there are new and exciting changes occurring with the Internet that are making policy advocacy strategies more efficient and effective. Keeping in mind the caveats discussed earlier, the creative ways that technology is being used to organize grassroots movements and simplify lobbying and advocacy today are phenomenal.

E-mail Campaigns and Web Sites

E-mail campaigns are probably the most widely used vehicle of Internet policy practice technology today. It is very easy to keep people informed about upcoming events, policy decisions, or to request action via e-mail.

For small nonprofit organizations or for task groups focused on a particular policy issue, e-mail is a cheap and quick way to get information to a large number of people. Many Internet providers offer e-mail accounts and basic web sites free of charge. Because e-mail and the Web are connected, one can attach a web site address that can be directly connected through an e-mail. Web sites can also be registered with various search engines, such as Google, for free. Although free web sites are appealing, your address can get buried under the domain of your service provider. For a small fee (I saw several between $7.00 and $10.00 a month) you can get your own web domain (e.g., www.stopthetoxicwastedump.com).

Web sites can be tools to disseminate information about your cause, your group, or your organization, and also can provide links to other similar organizations. They can be one-way or interactive. Interactive web sites are becoming more popular and advocacy organizations, in particular, increasingly provide direct links to decision makers on their web sites. One interesting example of an interactive web site is www.propeace.net. It provides listservs, blogs, connects to propeace sites in other countries, and has an instant message chat function. These types of web sites are not only good for policy practice activities, but also provide a source of support and communication to people who want to talk about the issues that the web site addresses.

The use of e-mail is becoming a widely used vehicle to communicate with public officials. Since 1998, when I first began to take students to the state capitol to meet with representatives and lobbyists, I have seen the interest in e-mail as an avenue for communication with legislators increase dramatically. In particular, over the last five years, when legislators are asked "what is a good way to communicate with you?" they always list sending an e-mail as one of their primary ways of communicating with their constituents. However, they also say they do not like e-mails that look like a group effort. In fact, I have had several legislators tell me that they treat those e-mails as if they were phoned in calls to support or oppose an issue: they tally them in order of support or opposition, but do not read them. Representatives are interested in constituents who take the time to write individual e-mails, not in forwarded mass form letters. This issue will be taken up in more depth in the next section on listservs.

Listservs and Social Networking

Online social networking involves connecting with other like-minded people around issues that are important to them (Satterfield, 2006). List-servs are a major source of social networking on the Internet. Listservs are e-mail lists that people join because they are interested in an issue. Listservs are among the most useful Internet power tools. Use a listserv in conjunction with your web site to push your message to your target audience and promote traffic to your web site at the same time. Listservs have many different uses and users:

- Associations use listservs to notify their members of meetings and events.
- Special interest groups use listservs to exchange ideas and discuss issues.
- Politicians use listservs to communicate with their constituents.
- Groups with members in diverse locales use listservs to communicate efficiently and economically.

Listservs can be one-way (sends out messages only) or they can be interactive. They can be unmoderated or moderated, meaning that someone looks at the posting before sending it out to ensure that it meets the guidelines of the list. One of the caveats of listservs is that it can fill your e-mail up if you belong to too many lists. Pick the ones that are important to you or your organization and that keep you abreast of your most-needed information. If you find that you are deleting postings without reading them, you should probably unsubscribe from the list.

Some of the listservs and e-groups that I belong to include:

- ETNPRONET, the East Tennessee Progressive Network, which keeps me abreast of local issues affecting my area through an online regional progressive community calendar and online information on organizations working for social justice in my area (www.etnpronet.org/info@etnpronet.org).

- NASW Tennessee legislative alerts, providing alerts for state legislation of interest to social workers, such as what committee a bill is in and who is on the committee to contact (www.naswtn .com/advocacy.htm).
- TrueMajority.org, a grassroots group that monitors upcoming legislation on a federal level (alerts@truemajority.org).
- WorkingFamilies e-activist network, a union-based group that monitors labor and family legislation at the federal level (www .unionvoice.org).
- Working Assets Flash Activist Network, a for-profit long distance phone company that believes in corporate social responsibility and donates 1 percent of long distance calls to progressive nonprofits of your choice (www.workingassets.com).

As you can see, my e-mail gets clogged sometimes. But I have chosen these particular listservs for a reason. I want to keep up with what is going on in my community, so the East Tennessee Progressive Network provides me with the comprehensive tools and web-based resources of its interactive progressive community calendar and organizational directory to keep East Tennessee progressives abreast of local grassroots issues and help build and foster authentic relationships between and among the community. The NASW list provides me with state-level policy tracking, so that I can contact representatives while a bill is still in committee. All NASW members in Tennessee automatically receive legislative updates on national and state-level issues. (Members can indicate they do not wish to receive legislative information and their request is honored.) The web site to sign up as a member is www.socialworkers.org. To view the Tennessee chapter's legislative agenda and key information on specific legislation, go to http://www.naswtn.com/advocacy.htm for information on Tennessee state-level issues, or to http://www.socialworkers.org/advocacy/default

.asp for information on federal issues. Social workers in other states can connect to their local chapter through the national web site listed here.

The last three listservs not only provide updates on legislation that I'm interested in following, but each one uses what Turner (2002) describes as *flash campaigns,* allowing members of the groups to organize quickly around policy issues as they are being debated. Each of these three provides direct links to decision makers on their postings. Because I am a member of each list, they will send me postings that already include my legislator, his or her phone number, and even a form letter that I can simply click "send" and it will be e-mailed for me. However, as I stated earlier, I generally change form letters (along with subject lines) into my own words, so that legislators will actually read it. However, on the federal level, most of the responses from representatives are form letters as well, so my sense is that the local and state representatives are more responsive to personalized e-mails than are federal representatives.

It is also very easy to start a listserv of your own. Yahoo, for example, provides free groups that you can join or start. But Schwartz (2002) warns that although listservs are easy to start, it is much more difficult to get people to join and organize around common goals. He suggests that it is important to moderate the listservs so that people who subscribe have common goals and want to develop strategies around similar issues. He also suggests making the goals clear up front and unsubscribing people who do not share them. Having managed listservs for many years, Schwartz states that people who are interested in working for policy change on a particular issue are not interested in debating it, but to connect with like-minded people to work for change. Unless it is a local issue that is gaining momentum but no one has already organized around it through the Internet, it is likely that an existing list can be used.

> **CAUTION**
>
> Online petitions and form letters are not viewed by public officials nearly as positively as an individualized e-mail. If you choose to use a form letter from a listserv, change the subject line and try to rewrite it in your own words.

It might be more helpful to create a strategy to organize people onto an existing list rather than to start a new one.

Whether you decide to subscribe to an existing list or start your own, the listserv can be used to accomplish a planned change effort, outlined in Chapter 2. It can be used to plan interventions without constantly trying to find times when everyone can meet. It can also include people who are farther away, particularly if you are in a rural area. For example, the East Tennessee Progressive Network utilizes technology to connect people from rural areas, but the issues are still pertaining to the local Appalachian region.

Communication and the Virtual Community

The virtual online community has taken social networking to a new level. Web sites such as Friendster and MySpace are designed to connect people who share common interests. Originally intended as a matchmaking mechanism for youths to find friends, these sites support personal web pages, blogs, and e-messaging all on one person's personal page. The web site itself creates its own directory of people and interests, thereby connecting people with what is known as a *friend of a friend* (FOAF) social network (Satterfield, 2006). When you find someone with similar interests, you can send them a message and ask to be added to their contact list, in turn allowing you to meet other like-minded people on that person's network of friends.

Although these sites were not designed to be political sites in particular, they have, on some level, taken on a life of their own. Nonprofits and others have learned to leverage them to accomplish political goals. MySpace, for example, is an extremely popular site that does not cater to a specific audience. It offers user blogs (an online diary of sorts, where people can post their thoughts on particular topics), message boards, and a free classified ad section. Nonprofits have begun to utilize the site to form groups (listservs), and use the message board to announce upcoming events.

But the most fascinating aspect of MySpace is the friend-of-a-friend format. Because it is one of the most popular sites on the Internet (from 90 million members in July 2006 to 120 million members in October) people can connect in a variety of ways. The most important way is that if you search and find someone who you are connected to or want to be connected to, you can message them and ask them to be your friend. If a person has 25 friends, those 25 friends' web sites are all on the first person's web site.

As I stated earlier, the site was never created for social activism. But it turned out to be an integral part of organizing the national pro-immigration rally that occurred May 1, 2006 (Melber, 2006). Known as a "day without immigrants," hundreds of thousands of Americans rallied on that day to protest congressional debate of a bill designed to crack down on illegal immigrants. *Business Week* magazine reported that the protests were so massive they forced Republican leaders to repudiate a controversial component of a bill that criminalized assistance to illegal immigrants.

How did MySpace have such an impact? The network of young people, in particular, that had been established to discuss social events took a political turn when people started communicating about the upcoming protests and national boycott of businesses. According to an article in *The Nation* by Melber (2006), messages spread among young people who had previously shown little interest in politics. There is really no way to tell how many people joined those marches because of MySpace, but the reporters who have written about it in the *Dallas Morning News* and *The Nation* found thousands of postings in a matter of months. One woman who was trying to get the word out about the issue acquired 400 friends in 2 months. This means that all of her friends had her web site linked to theirs, and all of their friends had friends of their own, so information about an issue spreads exponentially. Furthermore, because MySpace is registered with search engines, such as Google, anyone who searches for the immigration issue will be directed to many of the blogs on MySpace because it is such a popular site. The following Putting It Into Practice further describes this phenomena by describing how one activist, interviewed by *The Nation* in a recent article on the immigration issue (Melber,

82

Putting It Into Practice

Innovative Uses of Social Networking and Virtual Communities

Carl Webb, a self-proclaimed Internet researcher and political activist, has won the esteemed position of being the first "hit" on Google if you enter his name in the search engine. Why? Because search engines are currently based on popularity, and Carl has had many hits on his MySpace web page, among others. Surprisingly, Carl Webb has 10,000 friends on MySpace. Whenever Carl has something to say, he can go to the MySpace bulletin board and instantly send out postings to all 10,000 friends. I asked Carl how people end up with that many friends. "People want to be your friend because their page comes up whenever anyone looks you up. People can piggy-back off your popularity, taking advantage of a contact." In turn, search engines send out "spiders" or "crawl" through the Internet, picking up tags or keywords to use in searches. Because he has so many contacts, he can post bulletins or write blogs and these come up on the search engine. He decided to join MySpace to use the medium to get his political messages out. He said, "MySpace was originally intended as a matchmaking mechanism for younger people, but people have co-opted the space for other purposes." Has he been successful? In the last few months he has been contacted by the *St. Louis Post-Dispatch* for his antiwar views, *The Nation,* because of his immigration postings, and is currently listed under the Census Bureau's web site search engine. He said that was an unintended contact, because the search engine picked up his name and, because he worked at the Census Bureau, they automatically listed him on the web site. I wouldn't be surprised if he inadvertently helped promote the immigration rally, since he had 7,000 friends on MySpace at the time. *The Nation* article apparently thought so.

2006), has used the virtual community to get out his political messages, receiving quite a bit of publicity in the process.

Posting bulletins on MySpace results in an automatic message sent to all of your friends. In late December 2006 there was a story that was posted about a young woman in Iran who had been sentenced to death for murdering a man who had sexually attacked her. There was a web site with a petition that asked the death sentence be withdrawn and the conviction changed to self defense. My daughter received the bulletin from one of her contacts and reposted it to all of her friends. We watched the number of names on that petition increase to 350,000 in a matter of weeks. In the middle of January 2007 there was a final posting that indicated the petition, which now had more than 500,000 names listed from all around the world, had been given to the United Nations and an appeals court in Iran. The death sentence had been overturned and her conviction was reduced to a lesser conviction related to self defense.

Cell Phones

I would be remiss if I did not include cell phone use in the chapter on technology. The number of cell phone subscribers in the United States reached 159 million in 2003, and climbed to 180 million in 2004 (U.S. Census Bureau, 2004; Baig, 2005). More than 60 percent of Americans have cell phones, and it's not just for talking any more. Cell phones send e-mail, take pictures, connect to the Internet, and have instant messaging. It has become another way to access the Internet without having a computer; the instant messaging capacity was mentioned as part of the organizing effort of the immigration protests described earlier (Melber, 2006).

The importance of cell phones in being digitally connected cannot be underestimated, particularly because of their popularity among young people. It will be interesting to see how the rapid expansion of communication technology affects policy practice efforts in the future. Never before have so many people been connected so rapidly and able to respond to political issues as quickly as they are today.

Policy Practice Resources on the Internet

There are a variety of resources available for policy practice activities on the Internet. Rapid Reference 5.3 divides these into three categories:

≡ *Rapid Reference 5.3*

Suggested Internet Sites for Policy Practice Pursuits

Resources for Policy Practice Activities:

www.grassroots-advocacy.com

www.nfg.org/cotb/39resourcesindex.htm—community organizing toolbox

www.grassrootscampaigns.com/articles

www.candidateshandbook.com—buy or preview books for grass-roots campaigns

How to Find Your Legislators, National, State, and Local:

www.vote-smart.org/search/—Project Vote Smart

www.visi.com/juan/congress/—contacting the Congress (also in Spanish)

Policy Analysis and Watchdog Organizations:

www.cbpp.org—Center on Budget and Policy Priorities

www.omb.org—OMB Watch

www.census.gov—Census information

www.truemajority.org—interactive site for policy advocacy on progressive issues

www.urbaninstitute.org—policy analysis of social policies

www.brookings.edu—The Brookings Institute, policy analysis of social policies

learning tools, access to policymakers, and information. These are a small sample of the types of policy practice resources now available. Learning tools provide skills and methods for various planned change activities, including how to advocate on a grassroots level, how to run a political campaign, and how to organize communities.

Finding out who your legislators are has become much easier with the Internet. The two web sites offered in Rapid Reference 5.3 provide two advantages. Contact Congress provides a letter format so that after you search for your legislator by zip code, you can also contact them. Vote Smart allows one to search for his or her local representatives as well as state and federal legislators.

Accessing information on the Internet has provided opportunities that were virtually impossible just 20 years ago. Government statistics are readily available on any number of populations and social problems. Think tanks and watchdog organizations supply a plethora of different reports on policies of interest. Rapid Reference 5.3 provides a small sampling of what can now be accessed through the Internet in a few hours, in what would have taken weeks or months prior to the World Wide Web.

The Future of Free Speech on the Internet

No matter which side of an issue you are on, the Internet provides a truly democratic outlet for views of all kinds. The Internet presently has little control over what is published. With the inception of blogs, virtual communities, web sites, listservs, and e-mail, the Internet has become a vehicle for free speech. Currently there have been attempts to control the information on the Internet by broadband providers, such as AT&T, Comcast, and Verizon. Congress is currently considering a major overhaul of the Telecommunications Act. The Senate bill (S. 2686), like the House version that has already passed, would allow broadband providers to prioritize traffic on their networks. This can be done in two ways, through the speed at which broadband providers allow web sites to be accessed and through prioritizing access to their search engines. The bill does not bar broadband providers from favoring their own online traffic or making deals with Internet companies to provide faster service to their customers (Tessler, 2006). But Internet companies, including Microsoft, Google, and Yahoo! argue that providers could either favor or discriminate against Internet traffic without some form of protection of net neutrality.

The term *net neutrality* means that all users can access the content on the Internet without control or ownership of content. Search engines, for example, order their hits by the popularity of the web site, not by who spends more money. Although amendments were offered that provided clear guidelines for net neutrality, they have not made it past committee. Net neutrality language is intended to ensure that phone and cable companies cannot use their control over the broadband market to discriminate against online competitors or to demand a premium for fast, reliable access to consumers. Republican Senator Olympia Snow warned that the bill in its current form could turn phone and cable companies into the gatekeepers of the Internet, creating a class system of sorts between small, poor organizations and large, rich corporations and their access to speed and availability of content.

At this writing, it does not appear that this bill has the votes to pass in 2006. However, it is interesting that while researching this chapter, a new policy advocacy group, called "Save the Internet Coalition" emerged on the Web and gathered more than one million signatures on e-mail petitions, which they delivered to Congress to try to kill the bill or have it amended. Their coalition tagged onto the TrueMajority listserv to gather support. After the vote was tied in committee, the coalition sent an e-mail that said, "Although it doesn't look like they have the support, here is the position of your senators on this issue." They provided my senators' names, their position, and their phone numbers. One of the realities of legislative policy practice, which we will go over in more detail in Chapter 8, is that there needs to be support for an issue both at the grassroots level and at the lobbying level in Congress. Representatives need to see that their constituents are paying attention to how they vote. Even though big companies, such as Yahoo! and Microsoft, are working at the federal level, it is important for representatives to hear from their constituents, since we ultimately vote for them. This was a good example of using technology to get grassroots support for an issue.

SUMMARY

The technology revolution is evolving so fast that there may be a new, favorite social network by the time this goes to press. The ease with which computers can connect people from across the globe is unprecedented and makes practicing online policy practice an exciting prospect. However, the digital divide continues to widen—for poor and aged communities, in particular—and that is only in the United States. Thus, as with any planned change effort, using the Internet or computer in general for policy practice must be looked at in the broader scope of the systems we wish to target and the grassroots populations we wish to include in our effort. These systems will be discussed in much greater detail in Chapters 7 through 10. For now, it is important to see the computer and the Internet as strategies that can be used across target systems for a variety of strategic interventions.

 TEST YOURSELF

1. Go to www.yahoo.com. If you do not already have an e-mail account, create one for yourself.

2. Go through the web site at Yahoo! and look through the groups to see what kind of groups are already on the web site.

3. Go to the personal web site portal, Geocities.com, and create a free personal web page for yourself. Put in your favorite url web addresses when they prompt you.

4. Alternatively, go to www.MySpace.com. Sign up. Fill in the personal information. It will give you a web page. Fill it in as you like.

5. Click on the "my blog" and write your thoughts.

6. Pick a resource from Rapid Reference 5.3 and go to that web site to see what kinds of information they provide.

7. Go to either Vote Smart or Contacting Congress (Rapid Reference 5.3) and find out who your legislators are.

8. Using a word processing application, utilize the directions in this chapter to create a brochure or newsletter.

9. What are three potential consequences of the digital divide?

10. Describe what net neutrality means and give one example of what might happen if the Internet is not neutral?